PICKLES

Edible

Series Editor: Andrew F. Smith

EDIBLE is a revolutionary series of books dedicated to food and drink that explores the rich history of cuisine. Each book reveals the global history and culture of one type of food or beverage.

Already published

Pickles

A Global History

Jan Davison

REAKTION BOOKS

To Steven, with love

Published by Reaktion Books Ltd
Unit 32, Waterside
44–48 Wharf Road
London N1 7UX, UK
www.reaktionbooks.co.uk

First published 2018

Printed and bound in China by 1010 Printing International Ltd

A catalogue record for this book is available from the British Library

ISBN 978 1 78023 919 4

Contents

Introduction

Pickles. What comes to mind? The fiery kimchi of Korea? Turkey's *turşu*, with their vinegar tang? The spicy *āchār* of India? The salty *tsukemono* of Japan? Or perhaps it is Europe's sauerkraut and soused herrings? America's dill pickles? Or Britain's tangy chutneys? Pickles in their myriad forms are a global food. They are also a modern food. In the West, growing interest in naturally fermented vegetables – pickles by another name – means that today, in the early twenty-first century, we are seeing a renaissance in the making and consumption of pickles.

The story of pickles goes back millennia; the first mention of pickled vegetables appears in an ancient Chinese manuscript more than 9,000 years old. Throughout history, pickling has been relied upon both to conserve foods and add to their savour. In the Western world, 'pickling' is defined as immersing foods in brine (salted water) or in vinegar. Yet this is just part of the pickling picture. In Latin America, citrus fruits replace vinegar to create the region's iconic fish pickle, *ceviche*. In South Asia, pickles are prepared in mustard or sesame oil, utilizing the heat of the sun to prevent spoilage, while in East Asia, the art of pickling has been extended to encompass the ingenious use of various salty foods, including soybean paste and boiled rice.

Pickles encompass foods used as relish and condiment and those which serve as appetizers or side dishes. They are a food of great emperors and the poorest of peasants. Pickles were an intrinsic part of dining among the elite in Imperial Rome and medieval Baghdad. Yet throughout history pickling has provided essential foods for the masses. In ancient China, pickled vegetables sustained workers building the Great Wall; and in much of Europe, pickled fish, cabbage and cucumbers once formed the mainstay of the diet – so much so that the Lithuanians created Roguszys: the god of pickles.

What began principally as a vital means of preservation by happenstance also delivers assertive flavours. Pickles hit the spot when it comes to our desire for foods that both excite and satisfy. Through the centuries pickles have proved a welcome addition to bland, starch-rich staple diets wanting in flavour. In many cultures fresh pickles have been created specifically to enliven the daily meal. The Japanese prepare *ichiyazuke*, one-night pickles; the Chinese, *pao cai*, shredded vegetables steeped briefly in a spiced sweet brine; and the Mexicans, *salsas*, sauces of finely chopped ingredients, such as tomato, mango, pineapple, onion, chilli and coriander, flavoured with lemon or lime juice. Today, as the need for preservation through pickling becomes less important in the developed world, it is above all taste – the kick of salt, sour or savouriness – that gives pickles their wide appeal and their staying power.

In recent times, the health-giving properties of pickles has come to the fore. At its most elementary, drinking pickle juice as a hangover cure is common to many cultures. The dietary benefits of pickles have been known since classical times. The second-century physician Galen recommended pickles to counter phlegm, stimulate the appetite and aid digestion. Cato the Elder, in his *Liber de agricultura* (On Agriculture), advocated pickled cabbage, 'eaten in the morning, and on an empty stomach', to remedy 'disease of the joints', noting that nothing so purges it as 'cabbage out of vinegar and honey, and sprinkled with salt'. In the eighteenth century, sauerkraut, rich in vitamin C, was identified as preventing scurvy, the bane of every seagoing nation. Fermented pickles, produced through the action of lacto-acid bacteria, are probiotic: their consumption is beneficial to the digestive system, and it seems, also, to the lymphatic and immune systems. Some possess both anti-ageing and anti-cancer properties. In America, these associated health benefits have given rise to home and artisan pickle production, especially on the east coast and in California. The same trend can be seen in the UK, with the increasing popularity of fermenting pickled vegetables in the home. By contrast, in developing regions, food scientists propound that improved fermentation and pickling methods offer tremendous scope to maximize the use of available local foods and eliminate waste: in this way pickles may contribute to the fight against world hunger.

In this global history we explore the cultural and gastronomic importance of pickles from the earliest civilizations to the twenty-first century. We discover the art of pickling from ancient Chinese, Roman and Arabic texts written more than 1,000 years ago, to how pickled cabbage ended up in space. We learn of the iconic pickles of the East and the origins of familiar pickles in the Western world. Traditions and techniques have transcended time and crossed continents. The modern *escabeche* of Latin America has its origins in medieval dishes of the Middle East, while British chutneys are a lasting legacy of colonial ties with India. A common thread weaves through man's quest for pickles – a desire not just to preserve, but to create food with relish.

I
Pickling:
Principles and Practice

Pickling is one of the oldest and simplest forms of food preservation. The ancient Chinese pickled with salt, the Mesopotamians in vinegar. The techniques they mastered millennia ago are those we still use today. In this chapter we explore the science and practice behind the art of pickling. Examples of how and where different pickles are prepared are drawn from across the globe.

The Principles of Pickling

Fresh food deteriorates over time through the action of bacteria, yeasts and moulds. Pickling, which typically involves placing food either in brine (salted water) or immersing in vinegar or citrus juice, produces an acidic environment (with a pH of 4.6 or lower), which prevents the growth of food-spoiling microorganisms and eliminates certain food toxins and pathogens. In Asia, some foods are pickled in other ways, using various salty mediums or mustard oil, which we explore below. The method of pickling and whether the food is fermented as part of the process gives the pickled food its final flavour.

Pickling in salt or in vinegar is one of the oldest forms of preserving fresh food.

Salt has many functions in pickling. With all foods, salt draws water out of the cells through osmosis. This process firms the texture and concentrates the flavour, enhancing the taste. With fruit and vegetables, salt stabilizes and hardens the pectin in the cell walls, making them crisp, while delaying the action of pectin-digesting enzymes which cause plant fibres to soften. The presence of salt prohibits the growth of harmful bacteria, yeasts and moulds which cause food to decay. Conversely, salt provides the right conditions – moisture and nutrients drawn from the food – for lactic-acid-producing bacteria to thrive: these are responsible for fermentation and their role is vital in making many pickles.

Salt Pickles

Salt pickles are common to many cultures and are prepared in one of two ways: as fermented pickles, which have a long shelf life, and non-fermented, which do not keep and are consumed within a few days.

China is considered the birthplace of fermented salt pickles – a poem written there sometime between the eleventh and seventh centuries BCE describes pickling gourds. From China the technique spread across Asia. The Koreans took salt-fermented Chinese (nappa) cabbage and added chillies to create their fiery kimchi. The Japanese embraced methods from both, added more of their own, and today boast at least seven principal pickling techniques. In the West, notable salt pickles include herrings, cabbage (sauerkraut) and cucumbers.

Fermented salt pickles rely on the dual action of salt and lactic-acid bacteria. Together, these seemingly unlikely collaborators give pickles their characteristic texture, sour flavour and good keeping qualities. Depending on the type

Salt has many functions in pickling, from keeping vegetables crisp to facilitating fermentation.

of vegetable or fruit to be pickled, the salt may be dissolved in water to create brine, or used dry, relying on the fruit or vegetables to create their own juices.

Brine is used to preserve a whole range of foods. The world's most ubiquitous salt-fermented pickle is cucumber. This globe-trotting fruit, believed to have originated in India, is pickled in brine in Asia, the Middle East, Africa, Latin America, North America and Europe. Across the Mediterranean region olives are commonly cured in brine, and in Egypt, brine is used to make the country's popular *turshi* – pickled vegetables. In Southeast and East Asia leafy vegetables such as cabbage and mustard leaf are pickled in brine: Thai *pak-gard-dong*, Indonesian *sayur asin* and Chinese *hum choy* are examples. The brine may include sugar or be prepared with starchy water from rinsing rice; both methods provide food for lactic-acid bacteria and kick-start fermentation. In Malaysia, brine pickles known as *jeruk* include unripe mango, papaya, pineapple and lime. The sweet and sour flavours of the pickled fruits are popular with children who eat them as a relish. Bananas are pickled in brine in the West Indies.

Dry salting is used for vegetables that contain a lot of water, and is commonly used for cabbage. German sauerkraut is the best-known example. The salt is sprinkled onto layers of shredded cabbage which are weighted down. The salt extracts water from the cabbage and in a day or so it is covered in its own juices – these then combine with the salt to create the brine. In Eastern Europe and Russia, mushrooms are traditionally preserved this way and are a popular appetizer with ice-cold vodka. In North Africa dry salting is used to preserve lemons. The lemons are quartered, packed with salt, which forms a brine with their juices, and then left to ferment, often in the sun. The same process is used for limes in North Africa and South Asia.

Lactic-acid bacteria, which are naturally present in foods, are responsible for fermentation. They tolerate high salt concentrations and become active as soon as there is moisture, feeding on the starches and sugars released from the plant tissues by the salt. In the process the bacteria produce lactic acid, small amounts of other acids, alcohol, various gases, primarily carbon dioxide, and a mixture of aromatic esters. It is the acids, in combination with the esters, which contribute to the ultimate flavour of the pickle. Carbon dioxide, which is visible as small bubbles in the brine, replaces oxygen and helps preserve the colour of the vegetables. Two main groups of bacteria are responsible for fermentation. *Leuconostoc* species often initiate the process and produce a complex mixture of mild acids, alcohol and aroma compounds. Species of *Lactobacillus* tend to complete fermentation and primarily produce lactic acid. The dominance of one or other group of bacteria, dependent upon salt concentration, temperature and acidity, determines the pickle's characteristics and flavour. The differences between German sauerkraut, with its distinctive sour flavour, and Korean kimchi, with its low acidity and effervescence, are largely down to the bacteria present. *Lactobacillus plantarum* is primarily active in sauerkraut and *Leuconostoc mesenteroides* in kimchi.

Fermentation can take from just a day to weeks or months depending on the ambient temperature. The optimum temperature for the production of most fermented pickles is around 21°C (70°F): if it is too hot, fermentation is vigorous and a sour pickle results which does not keep. A slower fermentation, over two or more weeks, gives a better flavoured pickle and one that stores well. At room temperature, cucumbers undergo partial fermentation within 24 hours, although it takes several weeks for them to fully cure. During this time the cucumbers absorb the brine, their flesh changes colour from translucent white to olive-green and they become firm and crisp. Importantly, in gastronomic terms, the increase in the permeability of the cell walls enables the cucumbers to absorb other flavourings in the pickle brine, such as dill. Once fermentation has ceased, the pickle can be left in its brine in a cool place, or drained and placed in vinegar or oil, with spices or other flavourings. Brine-fermented vegetables that are stored in vinegar remain in good condition for a year or more.

Fresh salt pickles, made for flavour rather than preservation, are popular in East and Southeast Asia. The Japanese refer to them as *ichiyazuke*, one-night pickles. The vegetables are sliced, salted and placed under a weight for a day or so before using. The Chinese make fresh pickles, commonly known as *pao cai*, from shredded cabbage and assorted vegetables steeped for a short time in a spiced sweet brine that is kept for the purpose. Other light pickles are prepared from vegetables immersed in water and vinegar, flavoured with chillies, ginger or Sichuan peppercorns, or a splash of brine from the pickle jar. Similarly, Koreans prepare fresh kimchi with rice vinegar. In the United States, 'Overnight Dills' are prepared from fresh cucumbers placed in brine and kept in the fridge for a few days. The cucumbers retain their fresh green colour and acquire extra crispness through the action of the salt.

Vinegar Pickles

Four thousand years ago the ancient Mesopotamians were pickling vegetables in vinegar, a practice that continued to flourish in the Middle East and then spread to the Maghreb, to Sicily and Spain and from there to the Americas. Vinegar, with its high acidity (pH of 2.2), inhibits the growth of microbes and is a natural preservative.

Vinegar, with its high acidity, is a natural preservative. All types of vinegar are used for pickling. Grape or date vinegar is used in the Middle East, and coconut, sugar cane, palm sugar or rice wine vinegars in Asia. Wine vinegar, produced from grapes, is used for pickling in Europe and other wine-producing regions, cider vinegar in apple-growing areas and malt vinegar in regions where there is a tradition of brewing. Distilled or white vinegar is produced from malt or maize.

Vinegar pickling is common to regions where temperatures are too high to make salt-fermented pickles. In Iraq, a great variety of pickles known as *turshi* are prepared with vinegar. The vegetables are first soaked in brine, which crisps and firms them, and allows limited fermentation, and then covered with cold vinegar that has been pre-boiled with herbs and spices. In India and South Asia more widely, assorted pickles are prepared with vinegar, including gooseberry, pineapple, cucumber, tomato and bamboo shoots. In the north Indian state of Punjab, chicken and mutton are cooked with spices and pickled in vinegar. Latin America is home to several distinctive pickles made with vinegar or citrus juice. Cooked meat and fish, as well as cooked and raw vegetables, are prepared *escabeche*, pickled in vinegar, while raw fish and shellfish are pickled in salt with lemon, lime or bitter orange juice to create *ceviche*, now an international dish. On grounds of taste, rather than temperature, Britain has a tradition of vinegar pickles – its staples include red cabbage, onions and eggs.

Vinegar pickles can be prepared with undiluted vinegar, which prevents fermentation, or in a diluted form, combining a small quantity of vinegar with water and salt. Vinegar brines are popular in Turkey and the Balkans and sit between brine and vinegar pickles: the quantity of vinegar does not prevent fermentation, but encourages it, creating a slightly acidic environment in which the lactic-acid bacteria flourish. The vinegar also lends its distinctive flavour to the final pickle.

Other Traditional Pickles

In Asia, myriad pickles are produced without recourse to brine or vinegar. In China and Japan salty fermented foods provide the pickling medium. The Chinese favour soybean paste and wine lees. The Japanese, in addition, use soy sauce, rice bran, cooked rice and rice mould. The inclusion of starch aids fermentation; the lactic-acid bacteria convert it to lactic acid, giving the pickled food a high acidity which ensures it keeps. The ingredients to be pickled may be dry-salted or air dried for a couple of days to encourage moisture loss before being layered or covered in the pickling medium: they can be ready in a few days or require months or even years. In Thailand, rice bran or rice is used to pickle fish known as *pla-ra*.

In India, Pakistan and Bangladesh, pickles are prepared in mustard or sesame oil combined with salt and spices. The most popular pickle prepared this way, and exported the world over, is mango. The green, unripe mangoes may be left whole, stuffed with spices, sliced, grated, raw or cooked. Other popular pickles preserved in oil include chilli, lime, gooseberry, tamarind, papaya, jackfruit, aubergine, cauliflower, olive and fish. The hot, sunny days are exploited in making the pickles. Often the fruit and vegetables are salted and dried out in the sun before being packed in jars with spices and oil. The jars of pickles are placed back in the sun for up to one month, which aids preservation: the light and heat destroy mould spores and bacteria.

Russia has a tradition of pickling apples, pears, plums and tart berries, such as cowberries, cloudberries and lingonberries, in water with a scant amount of salt and/or sugar, and sometimes water alone. The fruits are left to gently ferment in their watery bath for up to one week. Their name describes the process: *mochenya* – soaked pickles.

2
Asia: Ferment and Fire

East Asia stands as the global powerhouse of pickles. The ancient Chinese were the first to realize the potential of preserving foods by fermenting them in salt and the practice spread east, to the Korean peninsula and on to Japan. Each culture made the process their own, developing new techniques and creating myriad pickles from fruit, vegetables, fish and meat. The number of pickles prepared is counted in the hundreds – they are part of the fabric of daily life.

China

> In the midst of the fields are the huts;
> Along the boundaries and balks are gourds.
> He dries them, pickles them,
> And offers them to his great forefathers.

Salt pickling in China is of great antiquity. The quotation above comes from the *Shijing* (Book of Odes), a collection of poetry that dates from between the eleventh and seventh centuries BCE. The Chinese word *zu* or *tsu*, which is used in the poem, means 'to salt and incubate', in other words 'to pickle', giving China rightful claim as the birthplace of salt pickles.

Vinegar had yet to be discovered. Another ancient manuscript, the *Zhou li* (Rites of the Zhou), which details the posts and duties of government officials in the Zhou Dynasty (*c.* 1046–256 BCE), illustrates the range of pickled foods prepared at this time, referred to as *chhi* (*qi*) or *tsu* (*zu*). According to the *Zhou li*, the Superintendent of Fermented Victuals was responsible for pickling, which now utilized vinegar as well as salt:

> To take care of the domestic needs of the royal household, the superintendent prepares sixty jars for storing fermented condiments and preserves; he fills them with *wu chhi* (five types of finely sliced pickled meat or vegetables), *chhi hai* (seven kinds of boneless paste), *chhi tsu* (seven varieties of coarsely cut pickled vegetables) and *san ni* (three kinds of meat paste still mixed with bone).

The finely sliced pickles comprised tripe, clams, pork, the root of cattail and shoots of water rush; while the coarse-cut pickles were of turnip, mallow, bamboo shoots, celery and chives. The pastes which accompanied the pickles were prepared from a variety of finely sliced meats including snails, frogs, rabbit and deer. These were mixed with salt, mould ferment and good wine and left for one hundred days.[1] Pickled turnip was paired with venison paste; water mallow with a paste of roebuck deer, and cattail root with paste made from elaphure – Chinese deer. Pickles were an integral part of meals in the royal palace, and always available for use in rituals or entertainments. The poem 'Xing Wei', in the *Book of Odes*, recounts a special celebration at which there were 'Sauces and pickles / For the roast meat, for the broiled. / And blessed viands, tripe and cheek.' From the duties assigned to the Grand Chef we learn that vegetables pickled in salt were used to flavour the sacrificial soup.

Traditional Chinese pickling jar. The lid sits in the trough, which is filled with water during fermentation to prevent air entering the jar.

Simple pickles were an essential food for the masses. Records from the building of the Great Wall of China under the first Emperor, Qin Shi Huang, in the third century BCE indicate that conscripted peasants, counted in their tens of thousands, were given rations of fermented vegetables in return for their labours; it is likely these included cabbage and turnip greens pickled in brine. The sixth-century agricultural manual *Qi min yao shu* (Important Arts for the People's Welfare, 544 CE), the earliest extant Chinese text on food, provides the first known recipes for brine-pickled cabbage and reveals the variety and sophistication of pickling techniques that had evolved from those devised by the ancient Chinese. Its author, Jia Sixie, details numerous pickling methods for fruits and vegetables, most of which are still in use across East and Southeast Asia. He pickles cabbage in brine and in another recipe with rice mould. He mixes wine lees with salt to pickle melons, ginger, bracken and pears; he steeps vegetables in salt

Sweet and sour Sichuan pickles known as *pao chai*. The assorted vegetables are fermented in a light brine with spices, vinegar and sugar.

and vinegar, and others in vinegar alone; and he uses brine combined with millet gruel and a mouldy ferment to pickle turnip and mustard greens.

The preparation of fish pickles was afforded great care. This ancient technique, which involves layering salted raw fish with cooked rice combined with flavourings such as dogwood, wine and orange and fermenting them in a sealed jar, emerged between the third and first centuries BCE. Fish pickles were consumed as a relish and their popularity earned them a special name: *zha*. In the following centuries, fermenting foods in cooked rice created all manner of pickles: pork, lamb, goose, duck, yellow sparrow, shrimp, mussel, clam and various vegetables. These pickles were beautifully presented – from the fourteenth century we read of fish *zha* prepared from the thinnest slices of translucent pink flesh arranged like the petals of an opening peony. By the end of the eighteenth century *zha* had fallen from favour, and only vestiges of this ancient tradition remain. The city of Changde in Hunan Province, southern China, is known for its special red chilli pickle, *zha la jiao*, fermented in ground rice and salt. Fish pickled in cooked rice continues to be popular in Japan, Korea and Southeast Asia.

The *Qi min yao shu* includes numerous fresh pickles such as Chinese cabbage, bamboo shoots, mustard greens and seaweed. Jia Sixie instructs that the vegetables are blanched, plunged in cold water, then mixed with salt, vinegar and seasoned with sesame oil, noting: 'they will be fragrant and crisp.' He also provides a recipe for a fresh pickle of wood fungus or wood ear (*Auricularia auricula-judae*). The fungus is blanched, sliced and dressed with vinegar mixed with soybean juice, soy paste, coriander and spring onions, finished with ginger and pepper. This recipe anticipates the use of *jiang* – fermented soy paste – as a pickling medium, which developed between the seventh and tenth centuries and is widely practised in modern China. Mushrooms, ginger, aubergines, seaweed and leafy vegetables, as well as crab, are pickled this way. The use of soy paste for pickling fruit, notably melons, pears and types of citron, has created a unique family of pickles, combining sweet or sour tastes with salt and savoury.

The importance of *jiang* pickles is reflected in the umbrella term *jiang yan cai*, which embraces the three main types of pickles made in China today. All have their origins in the recipes recorded by Jia Sixie. The first group, *jiang cai* (or *tsai*), includes soy paste pickles and pickles prepared with *zao* – wine lees and salt, which are common in southern China and the Yangtze Basin: *zao* melon from Yangchou and *zao* aubergine from Nanking are nationally renowned. The second group is *yen cai* – salted preserves. Mustard greens and cabbage leaves may be pickled this way. The leaves are blanched, semi-dried in the sun, rubbed with salt and packed into clay jars to

Sayur asin, mustard greens in brine, one of Indonesia's most popular pickled vegetables.

ferment, producing a sour and salty pickle. The third important group of pickles is *suan cai* – sour preserves, pickled in vinegar or brine. Among the most popular, and often made in the home, is *pao cai*. Cabbage or assorted vegetables are fermented for a day or so in spiced brine with vinegar, wine and sugar, producing a light, slightly sweet and sour pickle. The vegetables are removed as required and the jar replenished with more. The pickling brine is retained and refreshed from time to time. It is said the brine can be maintained for years, even generations, and improves with age. In southern China, the Hakka make *ham choy* from partially dried and salted cabbage leaves which are immersed in starchy water retained from rinsing rice. This method is used across Southeast Asia for pickling cabbage and mustard greens, continuing a tradition established over 9,000 years ago.

Korea

When Yi So-yeon, South Korea's first astronaut, blasted into space on 8 April 2008, she carried with her a special space-proof version of Korea's national dish, kimchi – pickled cabbage. The slim cans of kimchi had, reported the *New York Times*, taken three government research institutes several years and millions of dollars to perfect. The expense and effort involved underscores the importance Koreans place on their kimchi, which is a staple of every meal. Some forty years earlier, in a private exchange at the Oval Office, the South Korean Prime Minister, Chung Il-kwon, explained to U.S. President Lyndon Johnson the 'vitally important' issue facing his forces fighting alongside the Americans in the Vietnam War. The soldiers had been cut off from their kimchi and there was a serious problem with morale. Prime Minister Chung drew on personal experience to make his case: when he had been posted to the U.S., 'he had longed for *kimchi* even more than he had longed for his wife'. Johnson

Every autumn in Korea, families, friends and neighbours gather together to prepare kimchi from Chinese (nappa) cabbage. This annual communal event is known as *kimjang*.

saw his point, financing the canning and delivery of kimchi to Korean troops.[2]

To Koreans, kimchi, a mix of fiery pungent pickled vegetables – principally raw cabbage fermented in brine with radishes, garlic, chillies and other flavourings – has both dietary and cultural significance. Next to rice, it is the cornerstone of Korean cuisine and is served for breakfast, lunch and dinner, hence the proverb: '*Kimchi* is half of all the food provisions.' Three or four types of kimchi are offered as a side dish at each meal; their bold, complex flavours and crisp texture provide a welcome contrast to the blandness of boiled rice, porridge or noodles. Carl Pederson writes of his early experiences with kimchi in his *Microbiology of Food Fermentations* (1979):

> Prominent among the foods would be *kimchi* of several kinds . . . The first is so peppery that it may burn your mouth, and you hurry to the next which is mild and acid and not unlike our own sauerkraut. A third may contain nuts or a little fish.[3]

It is said that kimchi satisfies every palate as it incorporates the five essential tastes of sweet, sour, salty, spicy and bitter. The balance of these flavours is believed to increase energy and vigour and is strived for in every meal. For Koreans, the number five, based on the Five Phases of East Asian cosmology, holds special significance. Accordingly, kimchi should also include five colours.

Kimchi has been an important part of the diet of the inhabitants of the Korean peninsula since ancient times. Evidence of leafy greens pickled in brine and stored in earthenware crocks dates back over 4,000 years. From the sixth century CE, a stone casket at the Pòpjusa Temple is one of the earliest artefacts to survive which indicates the large-scale making of kimchi for winter – a practice known as *kimjang*. The collected poems of Yi Kyubo (1168–1241) provide some of the earliest descriptions of kimchi and the first known written use of the term to describe them.

> Pickled radish slices make a good summer side-dish,
> Radish preserved in salt is a winter side-dish from start
>   to end.
> The roots in the earth grow plumper every day,
> Harvesting after the frost, a slice cut by a knife tastes
>   like a pear.

The appearance and flavour of kimchi was very different to that usually prepared today; a fifteenth-century writer describes kimchi as 'a golden yellow vegetable'. Red chillies, which give kimchi its distinguishing colour and heat, were a later addition, brought to Korea around the end of the sixteenth century.

The principal kimchi-making season, or *kimjang*, is a traditional rite of late autumn and a significant event across Korea. The markets are filled with conical, long-leaved Chinese (nappa) cabbages and every family prepares dozens of heads for Korea's iconic pickle, *baechu kimchi*, calling upon friends and neighbours to assist. Public gatherings involve the collective pickling of hundreds of cabbages. Each cabbage leaf is spread with a thick paste of flavouring ingredients: mustard leaves, radishes, ginger, green onions, garlic, hot and sweet peppers, salt and ground chillies. The cabbages are tightly packed in brine and left to ferment for one month. The word *kimchi* is thought to derive from the Chinese *chimchae* – soaked vegetables.

During *kimjang* national news programmes run a daily price index on the cost of kimchi vegetables. A shortage of

Traditional Korean earthenware jars, called *jangdok*, are used to make Korea's national pickle, kimchi.

nappa cabbages in South Korea in 2010 saw the price of a single head rise from around $2.50 to $14.00 apiece. The soaring costs gripped the nation. The issue was discussed by the government. A leading newspaper declared the crisis 'a national tragedy'. In this instance, this was not media hyperbole. Kimchi lies at the centre of Korean life and religious ritual: it occupies pride of place at important feasts, such as birthdays, weddings and state banquets, and at religious festivals such as *jesa* – remembering the dead. Special kimchi is prepared for expectant mothers to ensure the well-being of their unborn children; and its communal making underscores the importance of family and community. The cultural significance of *kimjang* was recognized in 2013 by UNESCO, which added it to the 'Representative List of the Intangible Cultural Heritage of Humanity'.

Seoul's Museum Kimchikan lists 187 varieties of kimchi and each region has its own specialities. The majority are based on cabbage or radishes, seasoned with chillies, garlic and *chōtkal* – pickled fish or *chōt* – a thick sauce prepared from fermented shrimps or anchovies. Among the most popular are the archetypal *baechu kimchi* prepared from nappa cabbage, *kaktugi*, made from cubes of large white Korean ('Joseon') radish fermented with mustard leaves, green onions, ginger, garlic, ground chilli and other flavourings, and the soupy *dong-chimi*, prepared from slices of daikon served in its salty pickling juice, sweetened with sugar. Traditional white *baek kimchi* is made as it was centuries ago, without chillies: nappa cabbages are stuffed with mustard greens, spring onions, carrots and pears and fermented in brine flavoured with ginger and garlic. In the summer, fresh kimchi is prepared from a range of ingredients including cucumbers, aubergines (eggplant), summer radishes, watermelon rind and pumpkin blossoms.

The health benefits of kimchi are legendary. Scientific analysis of traditional cabbage kimchi has shown it is probiotic and rich in minerals, vitamins and antioxidants. Its

In the winter kimchi jars are buried up to their necks to maintain a stable temperature of 5–7°C, which ensures that the pickles ferment slowly. The kimchi is taken from the pots as required. Today, almost every home has a special kimchi refrigerator to replicate this practice.

consumption may suppress some cancers, cure bird flu and boost the immune system. South Korea's almost complete lack of SARS (Severe Acute Respiratory Syndrome) in the outbreak that hit East Asia in 2003 was put down to the curative powers of its kimchi, which saw sales to rise by over 40 per cent.[4]

The presence of teeming, fizzing microbes in Korea's famed pickled cabbage was one of the main challenges facing scientists working on space kimchi: how to kill the bacteria – which, when exposed to radiation, could ferment and bubble out of control – while retaining the cabbage's unique taste, colour and texture. Another task was to reduce the pickle's pungent, lingering smell. The scientists achieved both. Their efforts have seen kimchi not just take off into space but realize wider commercial success on Earth, bolstered no doubt by the

Buchu kimchi is a popular summer pickle prepared with *buchu*, garlic chives, flavoured with chilli flakes, fish sauce and salted shrimps.

Yeolmoo kimchi is prepared from radishes.

pickle's acclaimed health benefits. Canned kimchi with a long shelf life and less odour is exported worldwide.

Japan

Japan acquired much of its pickling know-how from Korea and China. It is said that pickles developed first in the snow country, in Japan's northern regions of Hokkaido, Tohuku and Hokuriko, where crisp fermented vegetables formed the mainstay of the diet through the fallow winter months; from here the practice spread. By the tenth century the popularity of pickles, collectively known as *tsukemono*, warranted their inclusion in the *Engishiki* (Procedures of the Engi Era), which set out Japan's laws and customs. The volume from 930 CE

Pickle shop in Nishiki Market, Kyoto. The city is renowned for its variety of *tsukemono*, many of which were invented here.

details pickling in salt, soy or fish sauce, wine lees, bran and fermented pastes, and lists pickles of abalone, aubergine, ginger, fish and winter melon, among many others. Over the centuries, the pickling processes were refined and extended to encompass at least eight principal methods and myriad others. For variety of pickling techniques, and the several thousand pickles that result, Japan leads the world.

Salt pickling is used to make the popular crisp nappa cabbage pickle known as *hakusai-zuke* and Kyoto's special *senmaizuke* – thousand-layer pickle, prepared from salt-pickled turnip with seaweed and chilli. Sweet rice vinegar is used for pickling spring onions as *rakkyo* and for *gari* – sweet pickled ginger which is eaten with sushi. Two salty seasonings are also employed for pickling. Miso, fermented soybean paste combined with sake, gives vegetable, fish and meat pickles a distinctive salty miso flavour. Soy sauce combined with mirin, a sweet rice wine condiment, creates a range of vegetable pickles from light brown to dark, salty to sweet: *fukujinzuke*, thinly sliced cucumbers or other vegetables pickled in soy sauce, is the standard accompaniment to Japanese curry and rice. Sake lees, the remains of the rice in the brewing vats, combined with salt, sugar and mirin or Japanese vodka is used for vegetables, especially daikon, melons, cucumbers and aubergines. The longer the vegetables stay in the lees the better: after several years they emerge deep brown in colour, with a sweet flavour and alcoholic bite.

Rice is also called into play for pickling. Boiled rice is used to ferment salted fish. *Nukazuke*, rice bran pickles, are among the most popular and are made in the home; they are said to recall the tastes of childhood, of 'mother's taste' – a pickled comfort food. Slices of cucumber, carrot and radish are buried in salted, flavoured bran for a few days, after which

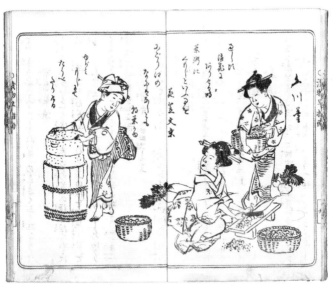

Making *tsukemono*, pickles, from a 19th-century Japanese cookbook, *Shiki tsukemono shio kagen* (1836).

33

they emerge crisp with a salty, tangy flavour. Less appropriate for the home kitchen, but common in every coastal community, rice bran paste is used to pickle fish such as sardines, herrings, mackerel and pufferfish. Continuing an early Chinese method, the Japanese also pickle in cultivated rice mould (*Aspergillus oryzae*), which is combined with salt, soybean paste or soy sauce. These primary methods of pickling have given rise to countless variations, often with seaweed or seafood added for flavour. There is one pickle made with no salt at all. In the landlocked Nagano Prefecture, *sunki-zuke* – pickled turnip greens – are fermented in the juice of wild fruits such as crab apples and mountain pears.

Early travellers to Japan found the selection of pickles overwhelming. In 1858 Lord Elgin led a mission to the Shogun:

> The Emperor had sent a Japanese dinner to his Excellency and when we arrived the floor of our dining room was strewn with delicacies . . . and when anybody made a gastronomic discovery of any value, he announced it to the company: so at the recommendation of one we all plunged into the red lacquer cups on the right, or, at the invitation of another, dashed recklessly at what seemed to be pickled slugs on the left . . . my curiosity triumphed over my discretion, and I tasted every pickle and condiment, and each animal and vegetable delicacy, of every variety of colour, consistency and flavour; an experience from which I would recommend any future visitor to Japan to abstain.[5]

Pickles became an integral part of the Japanese diet in the tenth century thanks to the teachings of Buddhist monks. The monks promoted a simple life centred on two vegetarian meals a day. Boiled rice with soup, a side dish of fish or vegetables,

Celery *asazuke*. *Asazuke* means 'lightly pickled'. The sliced vegetables are rubbed with salt or placed in vinegar, miso or salted bran for between 30 minutes and several hours before serving.

and pickles, which were already an essential part of the Japanese diet, became the norm. Then as now, the simplest of meals, *ichijū-issai*, comprises soup, rice and pickles. This can be pared down to *ochazuke*, a bowl of rice, doused with green tea and garnished with pickles, which is a popular way to end an evening's drinking. Tradition dictates that pickles are always eaten with rice.

The connection between monks and pickles goes further. The quintessential Japanese pickle *takuan*, prepared in the autumn from daikon radish, which is sun-dried and then pickled in salt and rice bran for two to three months, is said to have been created in the early seventeenth century by Takuan Soho, a Zen priest. His grave in the cemetery of Tokaiji Temple in Tokyo, where he was abbot, is marked by a

Japan's quintessential pickle, *umeboshi*. The plums are fermented in salt and pickled in their own vinegar before being dried in the sun.

large stone reputed to be the very stone that weighted down the lid of the pickling barrel. Most pickles have much earlier origins. The city of Ritto near Lake Biwa, western Japan, has a shrine built by its residents in the eighth century which they dedicated to pickled fish. Enshrined on the altar is a large salted loach. Loach *narezushi*, like most pickles, was devised as a means of preservation. Prayers to the gods were an insurance that the valuable ingredients would pickle successfully. The *narezushi* was prepared by layering raw salted fish in boiled rice flavoured with vinegar and sake, which was weighted down and left to ferment for up to a year. On feast days the pickled fish, pungent from their long ferment, would be consumed and the rice discarded.

Narezushi continues to be prepared around Lake Biwa using a variety of freshwater fish and is the precursor to the form of sushi which has become internationally known: bite-sized portions of vinegar-flavoured rice topped with raw fish, vegetables or egg. In the fifteenth century a way was found of shortening the fermenting period of *narezushi* from months to one or two weeks, which meant that both the rice and the pickled fish were edible: sushi became a popular snack. In the Edo period, sushi restaurants offered diners hand-rolled flavoured rice with a variety of toppings. By the end of the eighteenth century the original fermented fish had been replaced by raw, and sushi had changed from a preserved food to a fast food; now only the vinegared rice provides a nod to the original pickled fish and rice dish.

There is one pickle the Japanese set above all others, *umeboshi* – pickled Japanese plums (*Prunus mume*). This very salty, sour pickle, first documented in the tenth century, is held in high regard for its medicinal properties. The pickled plums are believed to act as a preservative and guard against food poisoning; in earlier times their consumption was said to pro-tect against the plague. *Umeboshi* is considered effective in quenching thirst and supplying salt and since the sixteenth century it has been standard issue in military rations. In each soldier's lunch box, a single pickled plum is presented in the centre of a bed of white rice, an arrangement that recalls the Japanese flag. The plums undergo a complex process of sun-drying, salting and pickling and it takes up to four years for the taste to fully mature. Their preservative powers may be to do with their own apparent indestructibility: they last, and remain edible, for centuries. The oldest *umeboshi* still in existence was pickled in the late sixteenth century.

The alchemy of pickling produces a very particular Japanese pickle, *fugu-no-ko nukazuke* – the pickled ovaries of the deadly pufferfish (*fugu*). It is said that a large ovary con-tains enough poison to kill twenty people. Moreover, the toxin is not within a discrete sac but found throughout the ovary. This unique pickle emerged in the late nineteenth century in the Chuobu region, central Japan. The pickling of

In Japan the salted ovaries of the deadly pufferfish are pickled in rice bran and malt, and moistened regularly with fermented fish sauce. The pickling process takes three years and renders the lethal toxins harmless.

the (non-poisonous) flesh of pufferfish had begun sometime earlier and was already a delicacy, yet the large grey ovary, often weighing over a kilogram, and with a dazzling yellow interior of tiny eggs, held the promise of even greater gastronomic pleasure. There was just one hurdle to overcome: consumption of the fresh ovary caused paralysis and violent death. How it was discovered that pickling would render the ovary harmless is not documented. Presumably there were fatalities along the way. That this risk was worth taking may in part be explained by the Japanese concept of *mottainai*: regret for wasting or discarding food of any kind, from fish scales to deadly organs. To make use of the ovary salves the conscience and amplifies its culinary worth: the diner can taste the respect afforded to it.

The pickling process is protracted. The ovaries are soaked in strong brine for six months to a year and then pickled in rice bran and fermented fish sauce for a further two years. They may spend a further month pickling in sake lees. How the pickling renders the highly potent tetrodotoxin harmless is not fully understood. A possible explanation is that the brine draws out some of the toxin and the lactic-acid bacteria break down and neutralize the rest. Producers dare not change their traditional methods.

Pickled *fugu* ovary, for those brave enough to sample it, is best served simply: with boiled rice and green tea. Professor Takeo Koizumi of Tokyo University of Agriculture notes:

> This savoury dish has a complex and rich sour taste, and a character that makes it hard to believe that it was once highly poisonous. It accompanies Japanese *saké* well, but . . . the best way to eat it is as *ochazuke*. This dish is prepared by filling a deep bowl about two-thirds full with hot rice, then adding a desired amount of crumbled *fugu* ovary over the rice. One then adds some grated *wasabi* (Japanese horseradish), sliced *mitsuba* (Japanese parsley) leaves, and a dash of powdered *sansho* (Japanese pepper). Finally, hot Japanese green tea is poured over the top. *Ochazuke* should be gently scooped into the mouth while the diner mediates on calming his or her fluttering heart.[6]

3
The Mediterranean: Ancient and Modern

On both sides of the Mediterranean, the pickling traditions of the past continue in the present, perfected and promulgated by the great civilizations: the Arabs, Egyptians, Greeks and Romans. Nowhere is this more evident than in that most ubiquitous of Mediterranean pickles – the olive. The techniques for brining olives described in classical texts are still widely used today.

North Africa

Shakespeare penned acerbic lines for the last queen of Egypt, Cleopatra: 'Thou shalt be whipp'd with wire and stewed in brine, Smarting in lingering pickle.' These memorable words may have given rise to the myth that Cleopatra attributed her beauty to a diet of pickles. Yet the ancient Egyptians left little evidence of the variety of foods they preserved in brine or vinegar. According to the Greek historian Herodotus, the Babylonians and Egyptians pickled birds and fish using 'salty sea water', a reference to evaporating seawater in pans to produce strong brine. A painting at the tomb of Nakht in Thebes depicts geese or ducks being plucked and eviscerated before being placed in the waiting amphorae. Similar scenes appear in other tomb paintings and an amphora containing birds preserved with salt was found at the tomb of Kha. It seems the pickled birds were consumed without further preparation. Herodotus in his *Histories* (II, 77) writes, 'quails also, and ducks, and small birds, they eat uncooked, merely salting them first'. Greek papyrus documents of grocery inventories and accounts from Egypt commonly refer to a variety of pickled foods, usually translated as 'pickled fish'. The enjoyment with which these were consumed, or otherwise, was noted by several authors, including the Greek satirist Lucian of Samosata: 'in the name of Isis, remember to bring us those delicate pickled fish from Egypt' (*The Ship, or the Wishes*, 15).

Whether the Egyptian 'cucumbers' the Israelites are said to have missed so much in the wilderness were pickled eludes us. Certainly in later centuries pickled vegetables, known as

Ancient Egyptians plucking geese, which evidence suggests were packed into amphorae and pickled in brine. Detail of a wall painting in the tomb of Nakht, Thebes, Egypt, *c.* 1400–1390 BCE.

torshi, have become an essential component of the Egyptian diet, prepared in the home and in simple factories where they are fermented in large earthenware pots or wooden barrels. Pickled carrots, cucumbers, cauliflowers, onions, hot and sweet peppers, green and black olives and the most popular pickle of all, turnips, their white flesh coloured deep pink with the addition of beetroot, are used as appetizers and served with almost every meal.

Across the Maghreb, *torshi* are prepared in a similar fashion. They share a common legacy – the Arabs who swept across North Africa to Spain in the seventh century brought with them the inherited culinary and pickling techniques of the Persians. Contemporary cookery manuals describe how various foods, including olives, capers, lemons, limes, aubergines and fish, were pickled and stored in large jars until required. One pickle of this region requires special mention: preserved

Assorted *torshi*, pickles, including the most popular across North Africa, pickled turnip, stained deep pink with the addition of beetroot.

Preserved lemons, pickled in salt, are common across North Africa and are a signature pickle of Morocco.

lemons. In the souks of Morocco, a mixture of fragrant *doqq* and tart *boussera* lemons are sold from large barrels, where they have been packed in salt and fermented in their own briny juices. With their distinctive taste and soft texture, preserved lemons add a unique flavour to North African dishes and are an essential ingredient of Moroccan cuisine.

Southern Europe

The ancient Greeks and Romans left us in no doubt as to their collective enthusiasm for pickles. The writings of scholars, physicians, poets, chefs and gourmets paint a vivid picture of the practice and pleasure of pickling across the Graeco-Roman world. There was little that didn't find its way into brine or vinegar. Pickles offered taste buds jaded by the daily diet of *puls* – a form of gruel – a welcome fillip. Columella, writing in the first century CE, advises his fellow citizens:

> Now is the time, if pickles cheap you seek,
> To plant the caper and harsh elecampane
> And threatening fennel; creeping roots of mint
> And fragrant flowers of dill are spaced now
> And rue, which the Palladian berry's [olive's] taste
> Improves, and mustard which will make him weep,
> Whoe'er provokes it; now the roots are set
> Of alexanders dark, the weepy onion.[1]

Add to Columella's planting list: turnips, swedes, cardoons, cabbage, chicory, lettuce, samphire and asparagus; butcher's-broom, cat-mint, horseradish, rue, parsley, thyme, savory and marjoram; vine leaves and shoots; plums, sorbs, cornel-berries and nuts, and we have a sense of the variety of produce to be found in the pickle store. Columella's treatise, *De re rustica* (On Agriculture), in volume III, Book 12, contains numerous recipes for preserving and pickling, commonly using one part strong brine to two parts vinegar. He observes early on: 'The use of vinegar and hard brine is very necessary, they say, for the making of preserves.'

To prepare hard brine Columella takes a wide-mouthed amphora, places it out in the sun and fills it with rain or spring water, into which he suspends a basket of salt. The basket is shaken and the salt topped up from time to time until it ceases to dissolve: an indication that the solution is saturated. The brine was deemed to be of sufficient strength when a piece of fresh cheese, small dried fish or hen's egg floated – a test still employed today. Vinegar was prepared from 'flat wine' and a concoction of other ingredients, including yeast, dried figs, salt, honey, fresh mint, toasted barley and walnuts, to encourage fermentation and add flavour. Fresh unfermented grape juice, known as must, was another popular pickling medium. Must combined with vinegar or brine was used for plums, the cherry-red berries of the dogwood tree (*Cornus mas*), for pickling roots and for fermenting olives.

Cardoons were given special treatment, preserved in vinegar and honey, so as Pliny the Elder notes, 'there may be no day without thistles for dinner.'[2] Turnips were another popular pickle. Columella pickles turnips in vinegar and mustard. The renowned gourmet Apicius indulges his countrymen's penchant for combining sweet and sour. In one recipe, he pickles turnips with myrtle berries, vinegar and honey; in another he mixes mustard with honey, vinegar and salt. These were turnips for the delectation of Rome's elite. The pickled turnip recipes of Apicius reappear centuries later as an early form of English chutney served at the court of Richard II.

One pivotal year-round pickle for the Greeks and Romans was a pungent fishy brine known as *garum* or *liquamen* – fermented fish sauce. The tenth-century Greek agricultural manual *Geoponica* describes a common method of making it.

Two thrushes pick at olives piled in a basket in this mosaic dating from the Roman period. Special varieties of olives were cultivated for pickling and were highly prized.

Small oily fish and entrails of larger fish were placed in a trough, salted and left to ferment in their own brine under the heat of the Mediterranean sun. After three months the pungent liquid was strained off as *liquamen*. While the preparation may not whet the appetite, it is how fish sauces of Southeast Asia, such as Thai *nam pla*, are prepared and we can assume the taste was similar. The Romans valued highly the complex salty flavours of *liquamen* and the best quality was coveted and expensive: Pliny observed that hardly any other liquid could command such a price, aside from perfume. The sauce was used as a condiment to add savour to dishes, as the poet Martial declared emphatically of a platter of fresh oysters: 'A shellfish, I have just arrived . . . Now in my extravagance I thirst for noble *garum*.'[3] Rather less nobly, the fermented fish residue from preparing *liquamen*, known as *hallec*, was used as a poor man's pickle: it was regarded as an ideal 'relish' to include in farmhands' rations.

A more appetizing pickled fish dish is provided by Apicius. Titled 'To preserve fried fish', the instructions are to the point: the moment the fish are fried, take them out of the pan and pour hot vinegar over them. Fish pickled in vinegar is prepared in Italy today, although for taste rather than preservation. The Venetian *pesce in saòr* is the best known, although whether its origins are Roman or Arabic, introduced via Spain or Sicily, is uncertain. We explore the history of Spain's *escabeche* and other pickled foods introduced by the Arabs later. There were other methods of preserving fish used across the Mediterranean. Greek sources reference mackerel and tuna in jars of brine; of pickled scallops and pickled venuses. *Htapothi toursi* – pickled octopus – is a classic mezze of modern Greece and is widely made. Its success depends on the care with which the octopus is prepared and the quality of the pickling vinegar. In common with countries of the Balkan Peninsula, the

Greek kitchen boasts a variety of pickled foods, a legacy of Graeco-Roman, Byzantine and Ottoman culinary traditions. *Toursi* – pickles – are an important part of the larder in the northeastern regions of Macedonia and Thrace, where every home has jars of hot and sweet peppers and crocks of fermented cabbage. Thrace is known for its pickled green tomatoes and the city of Naoussa for brine-cured grapes. The Greeks also lay claim to the world's most famous pickled cheese – feta. Byzantine texts are among the first to reference a soft, salty cheese with a pleasant taste. The Italian pilgrim Pietro Casola visited Crete at the end of the fifteenth century:

> They make a great many cheeses; it is a pity they are so salty, I saw great warehouses full of them, some in which the brine, or *salmoria*, as we would say, was two feet deep, and the large cheeses were floating in it. Those in charge told me that the cheeses could not be preserved in any other way, being so rich.

The Roman practice of preserving in grape must and flavouring pickles with honey and mustard laid the culinary foundations for Italy's best-known pickle, the sweet, yet piquant, *mostarda di frutta* – candied fruits in a mustard sugar syrup. Despite the similarity of the word *mostarda* to English 'mustard' and French *moutarde*, it comes from *mustum*, the Latin word for grape must, which formed the basis of the original preserve. (Mustard is called *sinapis* in Latin, *senape* in Italian.) Italy's oldest cookery manuscript, the *Liber de coquina,* written in the late thirteenth or early fourteenth century, provides instructions for the preparation of *mostarda*: 'take new grape must, make it boil until only one fourth or one third remains ... then grind hard mustard seed with aforementioned grape must, tempering it.' The *Liber de coquina* also includes a recipe

Mostarda di Cremona, Italy's best known pickle, with its jewel-like fruits, is a legacy of the Romans, who preserved them in grape must.

for *de composito lumbardico*, which signals the pickle we now call *mostarda di frutta*. This was made with chopped and blanched fruit and assorted vegetables layered in a jar and covered with *mostarda* flavoured with saffron, anise and fennel, tempered with vinegar and sugar or sweetened with honey.

Various types of *mostarda di frutta* are made in Italy. *Mostarda di Cremona*, with its assorted, colourful, glistening glacé fruits, is the most famous, and in part owes its popularity to its visual appeal. The English tourist Edith Templeton in *The Surprise of Cremona* (1954) described it as a *raffiné* dish, with fruit like semi-precious stones:

> There are several cherries unevenly rounded like antique corals, a green pear of the size of a walnut, with the black pips shining like onyx; a larger pear of the colour of rose quartz; a green fig clouded like a flawed emerald, a curved strip of pumpkin, reddish brown and veined

48

like chrysoprase, and the half of an apricot which could have been carved out of topaz. They are almost too splendid to be eaten.

Mostarda di frutta is traditionally served at Christmas, as a counterpoint to rich foods, and as a piquant relish to eat with *bollito misto* (boiled meats). In recent times the sweet fruit pickle has become popular with cheese.

Preserving olives has a long tradition in southern Europe. Olives were found in the wreck of the *Giglio* dated 600 BCE and were among the buried stores at Pompeii. Today they are the region's most ubiquitous pickle, cultivated and cured in a great arc that stretches from Turkey to Spain. All olives are green at first, turning black as they ripen. In Graeco-Roman times, special olive varieties were harvested unripe, for the express purpose of pickling. Cato, in his *Liber de agricultura* (On Agriculture), notes that *orcite* and *posea* are 'excellent when preserved green in brine'. He offers the recipe below for pickling in vinegar and oil, which is typical of many:

> How green olives are conserved. Before they turn black they are to be broken and put into water. The water is to be changed frequently. When they have soaked sufficiently they are drained, put into vinegar, and oil is added. ½lb salt to 1 peck olives. Fennel and lentisk are put up separately in vinegar. When you decide to mix them in, use quickly. Pack in preserving-jars. When you wish to use, take with dry hands.

Repeated soaking, often in seawater or brine, was necessary to remove the extremely bitter glucoside compound oleuropein that renders fresh olives inedible and is toxic to lactic-acid bacteria required for fermentation. Crushing or splitting the flesh of the olives facilitates the process. A quicker, modern solution is to soak the fruit in lye, an alkaline solution of sodium hydroxide; the Romans achieved a similar result by adding wood ash to the water, a method which is still used. Ripe black olives, with less of the bitter glucoside, were packed directly into dry salt to cure.

The second-century physician Galen thought olives to be beneficial to health. In his treatise *De alimentorum facultatibus* (On the Properties of Foodstuffs), he observed that those stored in salt brine and eaten with fish sauce before a meal purged the intestine, strengthened the *stomachos* (mouth of the stomach) and stimulated the appetite; olives pickled in vinegar were even better. A handbook of Greek humoral and dietary theory, *De alimentis*, concurred: 'The green ones that are conserved as *kolymbades* are good to eat owing to their astringency; they arouse the appetite. Those covered in vinegar are especially suitable as food.'

Olives were served plain or embellished. Cato dresses whole olives with fennel and lentisk steeped in vinegar. In another recipe, he creates a coarse relish: he chops olives and combines them with oil, vinegar, coriander, cumin, fennel, rue and mint, smothering them with more oil before serving. Columella provides a similar recipe for brined olives – suitable, he declares, for serving at 'more sumptuous repasts':

> Most people, however, cut up finely chives and rue with young parsley and mint and mix them with crushed olives; then they add a little peppered vinegar and a very little honey or mead and sprinkle them with green olive oil and then cover them with a bunch of green parsley.

The procedures for pickling olives described by Cato, Columella and others more than 2,000 years ago are still practiced today, although modified for large-scale commercial production. Spain, which experienced both Roman and Arab rule, is the world's largest exporter of fermented table olives. Over fifteen varieties of olives are cultivated for eating, with manzanilla, hojiblanca and gordal the most widespread. After harvesting, the olives are prepared as they have been for millennia: they are made edible by repeatedly rinsing, immersing in brine, or using lye or ash; then they are covered with brine and left to ferment; finally, they are transferred to fresh brine with various aromatics, such as herbs, lemon, orange, garlic and vinegar, which add to the flavour and character of the olives. The process from tree to table can take from as little as ten days to many months, depending on the olives and required result.

We owe the invention of the stuffed olive to the French. By the early eighteenth century, producers in Aix-en-Provence were removing the olive stones and replacing them with other

Green olives stuffed with chillies. The stuffed olive was invented by the French in the 19th century.

The buds of the Mediterranean bush *Capparis spinosa* are pickled as capers.
Botanical drawing by William Curtis, from *The Botanical Magazine* (1795).

piquant foods – pickled capers, anchovies, tuna and *pimento*. A
mechanical olive pitter was invented more than one hundred
years later in the United States. A California mechanic,
Herbert Kagley, devised the pitter in 1933 for the express
purpose of furnishing the martini cocktail with a perfectly
pitted green olive. More culinary lament than celebration, the
Californians also invented cooked, sterilized, canned olives.

The Provençal relish *tapénade*, made from finely chopped or pounded olives, capers, anchovies and olive oil, is a modern equivalent of the early olive relishes described above. It is named after the pickled capers, *tapéno* in Provençal, which gives the relish its distinctive salty, slightly bitter flavour. Capers are the buds of the prickly shrub *Capparis spinosa*, which is native to the Mediterranean region. They are picked before they start to open and commonly pickled in vinegar. The buds develop quickly and the bushes must be picked over daily, which accounts for their relatively high cost. Roquevaire in Provence is known as the 'caper capital' and sells pickled capers graded by size. The smallest and most prized, because of their intense flavour, are called *non parielles*; increasing in size and diminishing in value are *surfines*, *capucines*, *fines* and *capotes*. The mature green fruits of the caper bush, which are about the size of olives, are pickled as caper berries and are popular in Spain and Greece.

Turkey and the Balkan Peninsula

The Ottoman Empire (1299–1922) dominated much of southeastern Europe and Anatolia for centuries. The Turks drew in culinary practices and ingredients from across their empire, particularly Arab-Persian cuisine, and pickles, known as *turşu*, played an important role, both in the diets of ordinary people and in the life of the court, centred upon Istanbul. In the sultan's palace, the *helvahane* – confectionary kitchen – with its staff of eight hundred or so, was dedicated to making *helva*, sherberts and pickles. A selection of pickles appeared at every meal and the kitchen accounts reveal that they were consumed in great quantities. In 1620 more than 11,000 cabbages were purchased for pickling. Aside from cabbage, the cooks pickled turnips, artichokes, aubergines, cucumbers and gourds and numerous fruits, including lemons, bitter oranges and pomegranates, using the finest yellow vinegar of Bursa province. Speciality pickles were also procured for the palace: mint pickles from Bursa, grape pickles from Gelibolu and the most famous of all, pickled capers scented with mandrake, from Osmancik.

The thirteenth-century scribe Al-Baghdādī, penning his cookbook in Baghdad, could not in his wildest dreams have imagined that his personal recipe collection would, some two hundred years later, inspire the cuisine of the Ottomans, yet his *Kitāb al-Tabīkh*, which we explore later, was their favourite Arabic cookbook. The original manuscript is still held in Istanbul, in the Topkapi Palace. It was copied and added to through the centuries and forms the core of an extensive manuscript of some four hundred recipes, entitled *Kitāb Waṣf al-Aṭʿima al-Muʿtāda* (The Description of Familiar Foods). In addition to Al-Baghdādī's pickles, we find pickled grapes, plums, rose petals, carrots, cowpeas, eggs and small birds. The author assures us that pickled birds 'come out excellently'. Take six, 'fat, fine birds', split them through the breast, clean and season them inside and out with salt, mastic and Chinese cinnamon, pack them into pickling jars with a little brine and 'much salt', and then, the final instruction is to the point, leave 'until ripe and eat them'. The recipe for pickled eggs is more familiar: 'Take boiled eggs and peel and sprinkle with a little ground salt and Chinese cinnamon and dry coriander. Then arrange them in a glass jar and pour wine vinegar on them, and put it up.'[4]

By the mid-eighteenth century vegetables from the New World were an established part of the Ottoman diet, and sweet and red-hot chilli peppers had been enthusiastically added to the *turşu* repertoire. Recipes appear for stuffed

Turkish pickle shop where customers can pick and mix: cucumber, cabbage, carrot and chilli *turşu* are among the most popular.

peppers in a sweet vinegar brine, for 'pointed green pepper pickle' and 'boiled hot red pepper pickle', which is prepared with chillies and large quantities of chopped mint and parsley, packed into a jar and covered with vinegar brine: a mixture of salted water (brine) and vinegar. The low concentration of vinegar assists fermentation and gives the pickles an acidic tang. Many fruit and vegetables are pickled this way in contemporary Turkey. The liberal use of herbs was characteristic of pickles through the Ottoman period, although they are little used in Turkish pickles today.

The Ottomans paid great attention to the humoral and dietary qualities of foods, based on the teachings of Hippocrates and Galen. Pickles, particularly pickled capers, onions and garlic, radish pickle with vinegar, and beetroot pickle with mustard, were regarded as 'gentle nutrients' which aided digestion. Their consumption was recommended to counter the effects of coarse indigestible foods, of which it seems there were many; among them, game birds, most red meat, shellfish, octopus, squid, eggs and pulses. For this reason, pickles were considered an essential part of every meal. Round trays set with bowls of pickles were placed on the table for diners to choose as they wished. It was common to serve pickles at *helva* parties; their acidity countered the sweetness and high butter content of this cherished confection. Cabbage pickle was among the most popular, leading Sultan Selim III (r. 1789–1807) to pen a witty eulogy, which includes the lines: 'With joy and pleasure it is a perfect marriage / No helva party is complete without a cabbage.' There was one note of caution proffered in the dietary manuals. There could be too much of a good thing: an excess of pickles caused ageing and weakened the nerves.

Early dietary theory may be long forgotten, but the custom of serving pickles with meals continues in modern Turkey and may be at the root of many popular food and

In Turkey pickling brine, *turşu suyu*, is offered as a refreshing drink. The custom is common to many cultures. Pickle brine has health-giving properties: it is high in electrolytes, such as sodium and potassium, which help regulate body fluid levels, blood pH, nerve impulses and muscle function.

pickle pairings. These include bean stew, *kuru fasulye*, with green chilli or cabbage *turşu*, and grilled meatballs, *köfte*, with pickled cucumber or a platter of assorted *turşu*. In the Black Sea region, eggs are accompanied with green bean or white cherry pickles sautéed with onions. Cabbage continues to be one of Turkey's most popular pickles, together with pickled cucumbers, carrots and chilli peppers. Yet there are many others: sweet peppers, beetroots, turnips, aubergines, garlic and myriad fruits which are pickled unripe, including melon, apricots, greengages, white cherries, medlar, green almonds and whole bunches of grapes. Specialist pickle shops make and sell pickles for daily consumption, and pickle vendors ply their trade from pushcarts on the streets of Istanbul and other cities offering pickles as a snack and the pickling brine, *turşu suyu*, as a refreshing drink. The pickle juice from turnips and black carrots, *şalgam suyu*, is bottled and can even be bought in London.

The first Ottoman cookbook to be written in a foreign language, *A Turkish Cookery Book, A Collection of Receipts*, by Turabi Efendi (1865), underscores the transference and assimilation of pickling techniques across cultures. Efendi includes al-Baghdādī's recipe for vinegar-pickled aubergines, and there are recipes for other vinegar pickles. Yet two recipes, one for cabbages, the other for cucumbers, employ a very different pickling method: fermenting vegetables in brine, a technique first discovered by the ancient Chinese. Whether the Ottomans acquired the technique from the Far East, or if it arose independently in the Middle East, is not known.

Làhana Tùrshussu (Pickled Cabbage)

Cut the stalks off, remove the outer leaves of three or four nice white-heart cabbages, and cut them in four crosswise; then put a little yeast on the bottom of a convenient stone jar; place the cabbages over, add half a dozen of ripe capsicums, chopped fine, cover them with brine, put the lid over the jar, and place it in the pantry; pour the brine in the jar to and fro for five days. When the cabbage is turned acid, it is fit for use.

The Ottomans introduced their pickling methods to the Balkans and to Hungary. Vegetable pickles, especially sweet peppers and cabbage, remain an essential part of the diet, and in rural areas they are still made in the home; their shared origin is evidenced in their names: *turşu* in Turkey, *toursi* in Greece, *turshiya* in Bulgaria, *turshi* in Albania and *turšija* in Bosnia and Herzegovina, Croatia and Serbia.

4

From the Middle East to Latin America: Arabs and Conquistadores

This chapter is a tale in three parts, covering three continents and spanning eight centuries. Surprising though it may seem, a thread weaves through time and place. There is a shared heritage which stems from the court cuisine of medieval Persia, and a common narrative: one of military and culinary conquest that took vinegar pickles from the Middle East to North Africa, Sicily, Spain and Portugal, and from there to the Americas.

Mesopotamia

The ancient Mesopotamians had a taste for pickles. Among the world's earliest recorded recipes, inscribed on clay tablets some 4,000 years ago, are several which call for *siqqu*, a sauce prepared from pickled fish or locusts. The Mesopotamians used this piquant pickling brine to flavour their dishes; they made vinegar from barley or grapes, and they served a variety of pickles with their meals. In the city state of Mari, the grand royal palace of Zimri-Lim retained a pantry maid whose special duties included making pickles and fruit conserves for

Assorted olives for sale at one of the specialist pickle shops in the Mahane Yehuda Market, Jerusalem.

the king's pleasure. Were we able to step back in time, we would find the maid in the royal pantry preparing turnips, snake melons, chate melons, leeks, onions, radishes, hearts of palm, green beans, capers and olives. It is likely she pickled the vegetables as cooks in the region do now, salting or soaking them in brine before immersing them in vinegar. This practice was taken up by the Persians, Arabs and Ottomans, establishing a lasting tradition for pickles with an acidic kick across the Middle East and beyond. At certain times of the year, reed cages rustling with migratory locusts or grasshoppers would be delivered to the palace to meet their demise: they were packed live into earthenware jars and drowned in brine. Freshly pickled locusts, as we shall discover from later writers, were a tasty snack.

The ancient Jewish text the Mishnah, completed around 200 CE, almost two centuries after the reign of Zimri-Lim, indicates the enduring appeal of pickles, with instruction on when and how to pickle various foods, including turnips, capers, olives, leeks and locusts. Of these, the turnip, with its white flesh and crisp bite, proved the most popular. In Hebrew, the word for turnip, *lefet*, gave rise to *leaftan* – relish – denoting both pickled turnips and pickled vegetables in general. The consumption of pickles was to become an integral part of religious rites. The Talmud, the book of Jewish law, teaches: 'The one who is about to [recite the blessing] and break the bread is not permitted to do so before salt or relish is placed before each one at table.'

The Persians and Arabs: Iran and Iraq

This culinary epic centres on the richest and most influential city of the medieval world, Baghdad. The Arabs conquered the Persian Empire in the seventh century and quickly augmented their simple diet with the sophisticated cuisine of the defeated Persian court. This was a rich and complex culinary tradition in which the sour flavours of fermented foods and vinegar, lemon or grape juice were highly prized: tastes amply sated by pickles. The cuisine found full expression in Baghdad, established as the capital of the Abbasid Caliphate in the eighth century. Pickles and relishes, along with sour and salty condiments or dips, known as *kāmakh*, were an essential part of daily meals. They were eaten with bread as appetizers or taken through the meal to pep up the appetite and aid digestion. The Abbasid prince Ibn al-Mu'tazz was moved to write a poem extolling their splendour:

> Enjoy a wicker basket that comes with rows of platters laden.
> Assorted bowls of all kinds, red, and yellow, finely disposed:
> *Kāmakh* [condiment] of tarragon with its blooms, and red *kāmakh* and capers too.
> The noon sun bestowed them a hue, radiant with light from the sun they borrowed . . .
> Look at *kāmakh* of garlic and you see perfume enjoining you to eat.
> The olives as dark as night, put next to *mamqūr* [meat in vinegar] are shining with light.
> Look at the onions and marvel, as if of silver made with fire filled.
> Perfectly round turnips, subtly taste of vinegar, a gift of the generous rains.
> The white turnips and the red look like silver *dirhams* [coins] overlapping with *dīnārs* [gold coins].
> From every corner, a star glows like the resplendent light of dawn.[1]

How these relishes and pickles were prepared has come down to us in two remarkable cookbooks. Ibn Sayyār al-Warrāq's *Kitāb al-Tabīkh* (Book of Recipes) records the dishes of 'kings and caliphs, lords and leaders' from the eighth to the tenth centuries. A later work of the same title penned by the

Mixed pickles, *turshi*, are popular throughout the Middle East. The vegetables are soaked in brine and then placed in spiced vinegar.

thirteenth-century scribe known as al-Baghdādī unashamedly records for posterity his personal favourites. From al-Warrāq we discover a pickled shrimp relish prepared with apples and honey wine that doubles as an aphrodisiac, and a chutney called *maqra*, prepared from chopped turnip, quince, Levantine apple and citron, soured with a 'starter' of bread dough to encourage fermentation – a technique still used in northern Iraq to pickle turnips. We also learn how to pickle capers, olives and locusts.

Ṣiḥnāt al-Jarād
(Locusts Pickled in Brine)

Use locusts that have just been caught. Discard the dead ones and put the live ones in brine. When they all suffocate and die [strain them and keep the drained liquid].

Grind as much as needed of coriander seeds, fennel seeds, and [dried] leaves of asafetifa [similar to garlic].

In a big, wide jar, put a layer of the drained locusts, sprinkle them with the prepared spice mix, and give them a generous sprinkle of salt. Repeat the layers.

Allow the sediments of the drained brine in which the locusts suffocated to settle down. Slowly pour enough of the clean brine over. Completely seal the jar with mud. No air should be allowed to get into the jar, as this will cause the pickled locusts to go bad.

Now be patient and wait for them until they mature and become delicious and eat them.[2]

Pickled locusts were also a favourite of the ancient Mesopotamians. That a recipe for them appears centuries later in a medieval manuscript from Baghdad is not surprising. There is a remarkable similarity between the recipes inscribed on three cuneiform tablets from Mesopotamia written around 1700 BCE and those in al-Warrāq's cookbook, which is the earliest extant collection of recipes in Arabic. It seems that the food customs of the Mesopotamians, including the combination of ingredients and spices and their liking of vinegar, were acquired by the Persians. The Persians contributed their tastes and innovations, which were in turn embraced and elaborated upon by the Arabs – a culinary pass the parcel. This culinary transfer and synthesis did not stop there. The lineage of many pickles enjoyed across the Middle East, North Africa and southern Europe, as well as Latin America, can be traced back to these early recipes.

The scribe al-Baghdādī devotes a whole chapter to pickles, relishes and condiments, advising his readers: 'There are many kinds which are served among dishes to cleanse their greasiness from the mouth, to improve the appetite, to aid the digestion of food and to make food palatable.' *Mukhallalāt* – vinegar pickles – were made in great variety, using the profusion of fresh produce supplied from Baghdad's fertile hinterland. Al-Baghdādī prepares sweet pickled turnips from chopped pieces of the root, salted, spiced and herbed, and immersed in vinegar sweetened with honey and coloured with saffron. For mint pickle, he takes dried leaves and sprinkles them with aromatic herbs, bottling them with celery leaves and quarters of peeled garlic in 'good vinegar', golden with saffron. Al-Baghdādī offers the following recipe for aubergine pickle, which you still find prepared this way across the Middle East:

> Take medium aubergines and cut off half their stems and leaves. Then half boil them in water and salt, take them up and dry them off. Then quarter them length-wise and stuff them with fresh celery leaves, a few bunches of mint and peeled cloves of garlic, and pack them one on another in a glass jug. Sprinkle a little of the herbs and finely ground mixed spices on them, cover them with good vinegar and leave them until they are thoroughly mature, and use them.[3]

The Abbasids devised a range of *sibagh* – fresh relishes, usually vinegar or yoghurt based – to embellish grilled or fried meat and fish, which they regarded as too plain for the table. Al-Warrāq in his *Book of Recipes* credits the eighth-century poet and gourmand Ibrahim al-Mahdi as the creator of a simple *sibagh* to give pizzazz to fried fish. He soaks 'choice raisins' in vinegar, then mashes them, with 'a little garlic beat[en] in with the vinegar'. Al-Baghdādī prepares a fresh pickle of cooked broad beans, dressing them with sesame oil, caraway seeds and pounded cinnamon before covering them with fine vinegar.

Fish, poultry and meat were regularly soused or pickled in vinegar for keeping. A particular dish, *sikbāj*, which can best

Small cucumbers flavoured with chillies and dill are another popular pickle in the Middle East.

be described as meat set in vinegar aspic, is of great significance to our pickle story. *Sikbāj* was a favourite dish of both the Sassanian Persian court and the Arabs; its name is derived from *sik*, the Persian for vinegar, and *baj*, meaning stew. It was prepared by cooking pieces of fatty meat in water with herbs, spices and assorted vegetables to which wine vinegar and honey or date molasses was added, each to balance the other. The stew was finished with saffron, almonds and dried fruits and once it had cooled it was sprinkled with rose water. This elaborate concoction was served cold; its unique jelly form and melange of sweet and sour flavours was particularly coveted, so much so that the Persian emperor Khosrow I is reputed to have restricted its consumption to the royal palace. This dish, as we shall discover, was to inspire pickled foods of a very different form in Spain, Portugal and Latin America.

The pickles and relishes described in the medieval cook-books of Baghdad continue to resonate in the variety of pickles – *torshi* (derived from *torsh*, meaning 'sour' in Persian)

– which are enjoyed across the Middle East and North Africa. Now, as in the past, pickles are a component of most meals, served either as *mezze* or as an accompaniment to main dishes. Jostling for attention on street stalls and restaurant counters are jars of pickled turnips stained beetroot-pink, peppers, cucumbers, cauliflower, cabbage, onions, shallots, garlic, carrots, green tomatoes, olives, grapes and deep-purple aubergines stuffed with herbs just as al-Baghdādī instructed some eight hundred years ago. In most cases the ingredients are soaked in brine before being plunged in spiced and herbed vinegar, although turnips prepared in the winter may be immersed in brine and fermented in the warmth of the sun. In a reminder that culinary exchange works both ways, Iraq imports another of the population's popular pickles, *amba* – pickled mango from India.

Assorted chilli peppers, pickled in vinegar brine.

The Conquistadores: Spain and Latin America

The Arabs swept into the Iberian Peninsula in the early eighth century, taking with them their exotic ingredients and culinary customs. Surviving medieval cookbooks from al-Andalus highlight the continuity of foods and dishes brought from the eastern Islamic world to Muslim Spain, among them pickles and condiments and the esteemed *sikbāj* mentioned earlier. Spain's popular pickled aubergine *berenjenas de Almagro*, prepared in the province of Ciudad Real, is a direct legacy of this Arabic influence – the Arabs introduced both the fruit and the technique for its pickling. The aubergines, a variety unique to the area, are picked when they are still small and green. After cooking they are dressed with a marinade prepared from salt, garlic and *pimentón* (a later addition) and pickled in dilute vinegar. *Piparras* (slender green peppers from the Basque country), tiny cucumbers known as *pepinillos* and anchovies are similarly pickled in vinegar.

Dishes prepared *escabeche* – soused in vinegar – are common across Spain and Portugal, and are another pickling legacy from the Arabs. Etymologically the name is thought to be derived from the court dish *sikbāj*, although the Arabs employed numerous methods for cooking and pickling meat, fowl and fish in vinegar. The practice spread across the Iberian Peninsula as a way of preserving game, particularly partridge, quail, pigeon and rabbit, oily fish such as sardines, mackerel, shad and tuna, and in Portugal, small eels. In the process of assimilation the Arabic name became corrupted to *iskebey*, and from this it seems to *escabeche*. An early fourteenth-century Catalan treatise, the *Libre de Sent Sovi*, includes recipes for *scabeig*, *escabeyg* and *esquabey*, all comprising fried fish, over which is poured a hot vinegar sauce thickened in various ways.

Berenjenas de Almagro, pickled aubergines (eggplants), are a speciality of Almagro in Spain and owe their existence to the Arabs. They are prepared from immature fruits that are small and green, and are commonly stuffed with slivers of roasted red pepper and fixed with fennel sticks.

Spanish mixed pickles: olives, onions and tiny cucumbers known as *pepinillos*.
Spain is the world's largest exporter of fermented table olives.

Pex Ffrit ab Escabeyg (Fried Fish with Vinegar)
Take good fish and fry it. And then take onions chopped
small and fry in oil. Then take bread first toasted and
soaked in vinegar, and some flesh of the fish with spices,
and pound it well with the fried onions. Then when it
is well pounded, moisten with hot water, and put it into
the pan where the onion cooked and add a little vinegar
to flavour. Then when it boils, pour it over the fish in a
platter. And if you want, [add] some parboiled parsley
and also hazelnuts.

Other medieval cookery manuscripts show the pickling technique travelled beyond Spain to reach Languedoc in southern
France as *escabeg* and possibly to Italy and England. The term
occurs today in French as *escabèche* and in Italian as *scapece*:
both refer to fried fish in a vinegar-based marinade which

is served cold, typically as an appetizer. Once in the pickling liquor and refrigerated the fish will keep for a few weeks.

The conquistadores took the pickling technique of *escabeche* to Central and South America in the sixteenth century. The method was not only used for game and fish as in Spain, but was adopted to pickle vegetables, using vinegar fermented from sugar cane. A number of new and distinctive dishes were also devised by the Spanish colonizers. An anonymous cookbook of 1865, *Nuevo y sencillo arte de la cocina* (New and Simple Art of the Kitchen), written by 'a Mexican lady', provides a recipe for *manitas de puerco* – pigs' trotters with chillies and vinegar – which remains a popular *escabeche* and is widely prepared in Mexico and Bolivia. In South America the meat of the capybara, reputed to be the world's

Mangos en escabeche, pickled in vinegar, Oaxaca, Mexico.

Mexico's quintessential pickle, *chiles en escabeche*.

largest rodent, is prepared *escabeche*. A more conventional fish *escabeche* originates from the thriving colonial port of Veracruz, the second Spanish settlement of Latin America. Many dishes were introduced on the east coast and from there spread across the region. An early recipe appears in *Nuevo cocinero mexicano en forma de diccionario* (New Mexican Cook in the Form of a Dictionary) published in 1883. The fish is floured, fried and once cold placed in a pickling marinade of vinegar, garlic and assorted herbs. Similar fish *escabeche*s are found in Panama, Peru and Cuba.

A recipe book, *La cocinera poblana* (The Cook from Puebla, 1881), featuring dishes from Puebla, another great Spanish colonial city at the time, provides recipes for both catfish and thrush prepared *escabeche*, and another for what is today one of Mexico's most popular pickles – chillies preserved in vinegar.

Chipotle chile en escabeche
(Smoked *Jalapeño* Chillies in Vinegar)

Choose big chipotles (smoked *jalapeños*) and put them in
a pan with water until they boil lightly. Lower the fire
and remove the seeds from them. Wash them well and
let them drain and when dry fry them in oil. Prepare a
pot with vinegar, salt, bay leaves, thyme, cloves and cinnamon, all broken up slightly, and whole orange leaves,
and place the chillies in with them. Cover and let them
rest for three or four days so they soften well, adding oil
in proportion.

Preparing cooked and raw vegetables *en escabeche* is common
across Latin America, as is the practice of making fresh
pickles for daily use, combining chopped chillies, sweet
peppers, onion, garlic, tomatoes, parsley or coriander with
vinegar, lemon or lime juice. Fresh pickles became popular
in the nineteenth century and include the salsas or sauces
of Mexico and Chile, the *molho* of Brazil, Columbia's chilli-
hot *ají picante* or *ají Antioqueño*, and the herb-based relish
chimichurri, served with grilled meats in Columbia, Venezuela
and Argentina.

Latin America created its own pickled fish dish – *ceviche* –
which has been exported the world over. Ceviche is prepared
from raw fillets of fish, octopus, squid or shrimps marinated in lemon, lime or bitter orange juice. The acidity of the
citrus juice modifies the proteins in the fish, acting in a similar
way to heat. The dish is a speciality of Peru, from where it is
believed to originate, but is common across the region, particularly in Ecuador and Mexico. The classic Peruvian ceviche
is prepared from chunks of raw fish, traditionally *corvina* – sea
bass – marinated for several hours in freshly squeezed juice
from bitter oranges or the highly acidic Key or Mexican lime,

Ceviche, the national dish of Peru, prepared from raw *corvina*, sea bass, marinated in bitter orange or lime juice.

together with sliced onions, chillies and salt. It is served at room temperature, with pieces of corn-on-the-cob and sweet potatoes. A small glass of the pickle marinade may be served as an appetizer. The modern international dish of ceviche, prepared in the style of Japanese sashimi, with wafer-thin slices of fresh fish marinated for a short time and served as a first course, appeared in the 1970s. Its creation is attributed to a number of acclaimed Japanese-Peruvian chefs, including Dario Matsufuji and Nobu Matsuhisa.

The etymology of the word 'ceviche' is unclear. The eminent Peruvian geographer Javier Pulgar Vidal argued that the name is derived from Peru's ethnic language Quechua, and the word *siwichi*, meaning 'tender fresh fish'. Others say that it comes from the Spanish: *cebo* meaning food, and *cebiche* fish stew, or *iche*, small. The Royal Spanish Academy, responsible for regulating the Spanish language, is of the view that as with *escabeche*, 'ceviche' is derived from the Persian word *sikbāj*. Whatever the roots of the name, ceviche dates from Colonial times and the introduction of citrus fruits by the Spanish. How and where it was invented is undocumented, yet it is curious that *escabeche* developed on the east coast of Latin America and ceviche on the west. Ceviche may have been the result of independent culinary experiments, inspired by *escabeche*, or the consequence of trade between Spanish colonies. Spain opened up trade routes between the Pacific ports of the New World and the Philippines. A fresh fish pickle dish known as *kinilaw*, using vinegar rather than citrus juice, has been prepared in the archipelago for at least 1,000 years.[4]

5
From the Baltic to America: Sustenance and Savour

In this chapter we explore three iconic pickles of the West. We discover how the Dutch found the secret to pickling herrings, how cabbage was converted into sauerkraut and how the indigestible cucumber was transformed into dill pickles. These pickled foods became the mainstay of the diet in early modern Europe. Transported to the United States, they have in turn become a lasting element of American culinary culture.

Herrings

A fourteenth-century Dutchman, William Buckels, is credited with the invention of pickled herrings. Preserving these oily fish in brine transformed the herring's culinary and commercial potential. The abundant herring became known as the 'silver of the sea' and its trade helped shape the balance of economic power in Europe. The Dutch method was revolutionary. Pickling the perishable herrings gutted and flat in salt water, rather than piled in irregular salted heaps, excluded air, which meant they kept well. This advance was enhanced by processing the herrings while they were at their freshest, the instant the nets were landed – that is, out at sea, rather than back in harbour. Dutch pickled herrings acquired a reputation for quality no other nation could match.

The Dutch invested heavily in their new venture. By 1410 they had built wide-bodied, multi-decked ships, herring *busses*, for the express purpose of catching and salting herrings far from Dutch ports. These distinctive three-masted ships were the forerunners of modern factory ships. During the herring season, between July and December, they were able to stay

Joseph de Bray, *Still-life in Praise of the Pickled Herring*, 1656, oil on wood.

at sea for weeks at a time, maximizing their catch and cutting costs. Fleets of Dutch *busses* operated off England and Scotland in sight of the shore, outnumbering and out-fishing the small local herring boats. An English pamphleteer, 'Tobias Gentlemen', in *England's Way to Win Wealth* (1614) describes the Dutch 'gallant Fleete of Busses' working off Shetland:

> they do never lose the shoals of herrings . . . lading [sic] their ships twice or thrice . . . with the principal and best herrings and sending them away by the merchant-ships that come unto them, that bring them victuals, barrels and more salt.

The pickling process was highly regulated by the Dutch government to guarantee quality. The fish were gutted immediately after they were taken from the nets, graded and packed tightly head to tail in salted layers in wooden barrels. Each barrel was topped up with seawater, sealed and dated. Correctly barrelled, the brined herrings stayed in good condition for up to a year. In this pickled form, Dutch herrings were traded in every major European market. By the mid-seventeenth century the Dutch boasted a fleet of 2,000 *busses* and controlled Europe's herring trade. They forced the Flemish out of business, conquered the German and Baltic markets and supplied more than half of the pickled herring sent to London. Dutch-cured herrings commanded more than twice the price of those pickled in Yarmouth, Scarborough or Bridlington.

At the start of each season, the first herring barrels were raced to the markets by horse and gig. Their arrival heralded much excitement – the town crier summoned the townsfolk and flags were hung from the buildings. Herrings were a staple food of rich and poor alike. They were served straight

Dillsill, herring flavoured with dill, is an essential part of the Swedish *smörgåsbord* or buffet and is traditionally eaten first.

from the brine, or in well-to-do homes combined with other ingredients. John Collins in *Salt and Fishery* (1682) observed that the Dutch ate herring plain with oil, whereas the English chopped them small and along with oil added finely chopped onion, lemon and apples. In London it was possible to buy the mixture ready prepared. At some point in time it became commonplace to put the brined herrings in a vinegar solution with various flavourings, including peppercorns, mace, bay leaves, onion, mustard seeds, dill and, in the case of sweet pickled herrings, sugar. Sweden's popular *dillsill* – pieces of herring fillet bottled in vinegar with sugar and dill – continues this tradition.

Through the eighteenth century, the ravages of war and the deteriorating quality of fish took their toll; the Dutch herring industry faltered, ending four hundred years of domination. Yet the pickled herring had proved its financial and culinary worth, and it remained an essential food of the poor, peasant and labouring classes across Eastern Europe until well into the twentieth century. The Polish-French gastronome Édouard de Pomiane observed in the 1920s that the Jews of Poland ate a herring a day. The staying power of the pickled herring has been universal and it remains a common dish in otherwise distinctive cuisines. Pickled herring is an essential part of the Swedish *smörgåsbord*. In Poland, Lithuania and Ukraine, herring forms one of the twelve dishes traditionally served on Christmas Eve. Regional specialities have also evolved. *Sürstromming* – sour Baltic herring – has been prepared in northern Sweden since at least the sixteenth century. The herring is preserved in light brine containing just enough salt to prevent the fish decaying. The combination of salt and summer warmth encourages fermentation. The process begins in barrels and then in cans, which develop a characteristic bulge created by gases from the active, fermenting bacteria. *Sürstromming* is notorious for its pungent, overwhelming odour: its strong flavour is of secondary concern. Among its advocates, a *sürstromming* feast is one of the year's rituals. Writing in 1896, the Swedish gastronome Charles Emil Hagdahl had this to say:

> *Sürstromming* is eaten only by the initiated, au naturel, without any other sauce than that the mouth waters. They consider it a delicacy of the most sublime kind; but it will never become a festive food, unless the host prefers to eat alone, or maybe chooses guests who have no nose.[1]

By contrast, 'maiden herring' – *matjes* in German and Swedish, *maatjes* in Dutch – are a popular form of lightly pickled herrings. The young fish, caught before they have spawned, are partially gutted and pickled in a mild salt-brine for around five days. The pancreas is left in place, releasing enzymes during curing which gives the *matjes* its characteristic mild flavour and soft texture. In Central Europe, the young fish are prepared as *schmaltz* herring. *Schmaltz*, which means fat in Yiddish, reflects the strong association of East European Jewish cuisine with herrings. The fish are caught when they are at their fattest, gutted and salted whole in barrels. To serve, the herrings are soaked to rid them of salt, filleted, then marinated in vegetable oil, vinaigrette or sour cream. Early nineteenth-century Berlin is credited with the creation of *Rollmöpse* – rollmops. The brined herring fillets are wrapped around pickled cucumber, fixed with wooden skewers, packed into jars and covered with spiced vinegar. Prince Otto von

Schmaltz herring, pickled in brine and then marinated in vinaigrette, vegetable oil or sour cream, has its origins in Eastern Europe.

Bismarck, founder of the German Reich, lent his name to the Bismarck herring, fillets marinated in vinegar with onion rings and spices. Bismarck is reputed to have remarked: 'If only herring were as costly as caviar and oysters, it would be considered a rare delicacy.'

Pickled Cucumbers

It took some time for Europe to realize the gastronomic potential of the cucumber. The bitter-tasting ovoid fruits from India, known to the Romans in the first century CE, spread slowly across the continent, reaching France by the ninth century. The cucumber's slow passage north may be explained by its perceived want of culinary merit: consumption seemed to offer little reward to the diner but indigestion and flatulence. The English, who came to know the cucumber

Cucumbers are the most popular of all pickled vegetables and are prepared across the globe.

only in the fourteenth century, were particularly scathing. John Evelyn writing in 1699 recounts that the cucumber, 'however dress'd, was thought fit to be thrown away, being accounted little better than poyson'.[2] Exactly when cucumbers were first pickled in brine is uncertain, but the act was transformative. The process of lacto-acid fermentation, facilitated by the salt brine, improved the digestibility of cucumbers and their flavour. Above all, the cucumbers kept well.

Brine-pickled cucumbers, along with sauerkraut, became a staple food of early modern Europe, especially in central, northern and eastern regions. Families prepared barrels of cucumbers, along with cabbages, beetroots and mushrooms, to see them through the winter – their sharp flavour was a valued addition to the basic diet of bread and potatoes. Elena Molokhovets in *A Gift to Young Housewives*, the most successful Russian cookbook of the nineteenth century, offers several recipes for pickled cucumbers, including the following:

Solenye Ogurtsy (Salted Cucumbers)

Dry out very clean river sand and pass it through a fine sieve. Spread a layer of this sand, the thickness of your palm, on the bottom of a barrel. Add a layer of clean black currant leaves, dill, and horseradish cut into pieces, followed by a layer of cucumbers. Cover the cucumbers with another layer of leaves, dill and horseradish, topped with a layer of sand. Continue in this manner until the barrel is full. The last layer over the cucumbers must be currant leaves, with sand on the very top. Prepare the brine as follows: For one pail of water use one and a half pounds of salt. Bring to the boil, cool, and cover the cucumbers completely with the brine. Replenish the brine as it evaporates. Before any kind of salting, cucumbers must be soaked for 12–15 hours in water with ice.

Molokhovets's use of blackcurrant leaves highlights the principal challenge when pickling cucumbers – how to keep them crisp. Blackcurrant leaves have a high concentration of tannic acid, which helps retain the rigidity of the cucumbers' cell walls and so their crunch. In Russia, pickle bouquets garnis are sold in the markets for flavouring cucumbers. Umbels of dill, horseradish leaves and shoots of garlic are tied together, often with blackcurrant, cherry or oak leaves; and in the south with fresh bay and grape leaves, which possess similarly high tannin levels. 'Pickling lime' or alum (aluminium hydroxide) work in the same way.

Over time, special varieties of short or dwarf cucumbers, known as gherkins in English, were developed for the express purpose of pickling. The French went a stage further and developed tiny fruited cucumbers, no larger than a child's finger, which go under the name *cornichons*.

Sauerkraut

In the history of pickles, sauerkraut, as it is made today, is a relative newcomer – no more than four hundred years old. The distinguishing feature of sauerkraut is that it is dry salted. Other cabbage pickles, such as those perfected by the Chinese millennia ago, are prepared 'wet', by adding brine to the cabbage. For sauerkraut, dry salt is sprinkled onto the shredded cabbage, which is firmly weighted down. Within a short amount of time the cabbage gives up sufficient moisture to create its own brine and fermentation begins. This innovation, which Europe can claim as its own, was arrived at by degrees.

The Romans pickled cabbage in brine and vinegar. In the Middle Ages, cabbage was cut into pieces, packed in crocks and covered with verjuice, sour wine or vinegar, to which

Sauerkraut, or pickled cabbage, is a European invention.

great quantities of salt was added. Contemporary accounts describe how the French prepared cabbages this way. The highly acidic and salty liquids preserved the vegetables but had limitations. Significant quantities of vinegar or verjuice were required for pickling, while the sourness and saltiness of the pickled cabbage meant it required soaking in plain water before use. The German name of *Sauerkraut*, literally 'sour cabbage', may be indicative of the predominant taste of these early cabbage pickles: the name, long in use, continued after the technique changed.

At some point the sour liquids were dropped and in their place brine was added to the pickling barrel. This development reduced the sourness of the pickle liquor and facilitated lacto-fermentation, which much improved the cabbage's flavour. One of the earliest accounts of preserving cabbage in brine is provided in *Le Thresor de Santi*, published in 1607, which describes how Germans prepared cabbage for winter use. The cabbages were shredded and placed in layers with salt, juniper berries, spices, barberries and pepper. Each layer was pressed down firmly and brine added. By the time Hannah Glasse came to include a recipe for 'Sour Crout' in her 1758 edition of *The Art of Cookery Made Plain and Easy*, the method of dry salting was well established. She notes: 'It is a dish much made use of amongst the Germans and in the North Countries, where the Frost kills all the cabbages.' The hard, white cabbages were pickled whole, with a large handful of salt to every four or five heads and pounded caraway seeds to give a 'fine flavour'. Once salted, the cabbages were

Red cabbage, shredded and sprinkled with salt, before being naturally fermented as sauerkraut.

St Nicholas Saving Three Children from the Pickle Barrel, late 15th–16th century, limestone, Swabia, Germany. Based on the story of St Nicholas restoring the children to life after an innkeeper murdered them to pickle and feed to his guests.

weighted down, covered closely and left to stand for a month before using.

Pickled cabbage was a mainstay of much of Europe. In Poland, it was customary to pickle cabbages in board-clad earthen pits, a practice that continued until the mid-twentieth century. Layers of whole cabbages were alternated with layers of finely shredded leaves, with or without salt, depending on the finances of the family, and covered and weighted down with heavy stones. Preserving with little or no salt produces soft cabbage with little flavour; dill and caraway seeds were added to compensate, and in some districts oak and cherry leaves were layered with the cabbages: the tannic acid in the leaves helped to keep them crisp.

Sauerkraut came to greater prominence in Britain through James Lind and his pioneering work on the prevention of scurvy, the scourge of every navy at this time. In the third edition of his famous *A Treatise on the Scurvy*, published in 1772, Lind describes in detail the Dutch method of making *zourkool* – sour cabbage. The white winter cabbages were shaved into fine slices and layered with salt in wooden barrels prepared with a lining of grease and flour paste to limit contact with the air. A tight wooden cover compressed the cabbages to form the brine. After two to four weeks fermentation was complete. The sour liquid which seeped out at the top of the cask was removed and replaced with fresh water, which kept the cask airtight. In this way the cabbage lasted well, as Lind observed: 'I sent a small cask to Newfoundland, and eight months afterwards had part of them returned to me good and well relished.' The keeping qualities of the cabbage were paramount: Lind noted that Dutch sailors were less liable to scurvy, 'owing to this pickled vegetable carried to sea'. Two helpings a week were all that was required.

Captain Cook, widely credited with winning the battle against scurvy on long voyages, attributed his success in part to persuading his reluctant crew to eat 'sour crout'. When at first they refused, Cook, knowing his men's dislike of anything 'out of the common way, altho it be ever so much for their good', ordered the cabbage be served only to the officers, for when 'their superiors set a Value on it, it becomes the finest stuff in the World'. We know now that sauerkraut's effectiveness in preventing scurvy is down to the high levels of vitamin C in fresh cabbage, much of which is preserved through pickling. The process of making *zourkool* described by Lind is, to all intents and purposes, how sauerkraut is prepared today, typically using mild-flavoured, hard white cabbages. Whether the dry salting method was developed first in Germany, the Netherlands or elsewhere, the German name of 'sauerkraut', also adopted into English, and adapted by the French as *choucroute*, strongly links its heritage and invention with Germany. The nineteenth-century German poet Ludwig Uhland claimed as much:

> Also our noble sauerkraut,
> We should not forget it;
> A German first created it,
> Therefore it's a German dish.
> If such a little piece of meat, white and mild,
> Lies in kraut that is a picture
> As Venus in the roses.[3]

Variations of sauerkraut exist across modern Europe, eaten cooked or raw, hot or cold, plain or embellished. The Russians, Ukrainians and Belarusians pickle their cabbage with shredded carrots. The Poles flavour the cabbage with onions and garlic and add red beetroot for colour. In the Balkans, it is common to pickle whole cabbage heads; they may be coloured pink by adding beetroot, or amber by including quince. The Serbians pickle red cabbage in the same way and enjoy the pink brine as a drink. Sauerkraut was taken to America by German and Polish immigrants in the nineteenth century and it soon became a standard provision in every delicatessen.

North America

Very few foods escaped the pickling crock in early America. European settlers brought with them fruits and vegetables to cultivate and their culinary practices for preserving them, providing a legacy of brined cucumbers and vinegar pickles, salt beef and sauerkraut. English-speaking colonies took their cue from Britain. Martha Washington's manuscript cookbook, with recipes dating from sixteenth-century Virginia, includes instructions for pickling asparagus, broom buds, barberries, lettuce stalks and flowers; there is soused pike and eel, pickled cockles and mussels and barrelled oysters: ingredients and methods familiar to every English cook. Notably, two recipes are given for pickled cucumbers, and it is evident that these were prepared on a large scale: one instructs to add '2 penny of allom' to every hundred cucumbers to ensure they remain 'crump and green'.

Cucumbers quickly became the quintessential American pickle. They arrived in North America with the Spanish. Christopher Columbus took them to Hispaniola in the 1490s and less than a century later, cucumbers were being grown by Native American peoples in Montreal, New York, Virginia, Florida and the Great Plains. The settlers soon joined them. In 1659 Dutch farmers began to cultivate cucumbers on Long Island, in the area now known as Brooklyn. Soon New York City boasted the largest concentration of commercial picklers in America and cured cucumbers were sold from market stalls on Washington, Canal and Fulton streets. Their popularity led to the cucumber becoming synonymous with the term 'pickle'. Thomas Jefferson is reputed to have said: 'On a hot day in Virginia, I know of nothing more comforting than a fine spiced pickle, brought up trout-like from the sparkling depths of the aromatic jar below the stairs of Aunt Sally's cellar.'

Tomatoes were among a panoply of foods pickled in early America; other popular pickles included cucumbers, peaches and bell peppers.

American cooks were kept busy through the growing season pickling, bottling, canning and preparing jams, chutneys and 'store sauces' such as catsups and ketchups. Miss Eliza Leslie, author of *Directions for Cookery, in its Various Branches* (1840), one of the most popular American cookbooks of the period, provides numerous pickle recipes including foods common to the Americas, soft-shelled butternuts (white walnuts), bell peppers, peaches and 'tomatas', which she salts and pickles in water and vinegar. Regional pickles also appear in print. Mary Randolph in *The Virginia Housewife* (1838) includes 'yellow pickles', probably inspired by English piccalilli, coloured with turmeric and hotly spiced with ginger, horseradish and mustard seed. Recipes for chow chow, a sweet mustard pickle of mixed vegetables, another speciality of the southern United States (and popular along the east coast of Canada), appear in Marion Cabell Tyree's classic, *Housekeeping in Old Virginia* (1878), a compilation of 1,700 'favorite recipes from 250 famous families of Virginia'. How the pickle acquired its name is not known. The vegetables are pickled raw or more commonly, as now, cooked in spiced vinegar which is generously sweetened with brown sugar. The following recipe, which was contributed by 'Mrs C. N.', is a typical example.

Chow Chow

½ peck onions.
½ peck green tomatoes.
3 dozen large cucumbers.
4 large green peppers.
½ pint small peppers, red and green.

Sprinkle one pint salt on, and let them stand all night; the cucumbers not peeled, but sliced one inch thick, the onions also sliced.

In the morning drain off the brine, and add to the pickles: 1 oz mace; 1 oz black pepper; 1 oz white mustard-seed; 1 oz turmeric; ½ oz cloves; ½ oz celery-seed; 3 tbsp made mustard; 2 lbs brown sugar; a little horseradish.

Cover [the pickles] with vinegar, and boil till tender,
a half-hour or more. When cold, ready for use.

Across the United States pickles were a regular feature at mealtimes. The English writer Frances Trollope, in her travelogue *Domestic Manners of the Americans* (1832), describes a tea party in Cincinnati in the 1820s, where, along with assorted cakes, guests were offered 'pickled peaches and preserved cucumbers, ham, turkey, hung beef, apple sauce, and pickled oysters'. Pickles were also to become part of Thanksgiving dinner. Sarah Josepha Hale, author and social activist, who campaigned to make Thanksgiving a national holiday, first expressed her idea in the novel *Northwood* (1827). The character Squire Romilly sits down to Thanksgiving dinner with roast turkey as its centrepiece, surrounded by, among other things, pickles and preserves. The china for this special meal would have matched: a full dinner service included a complement of pickle dishes. A Thanksgiving menu from 1870 continues the pickles custom, which endures in many American homes today – roast turkey is accompanied by cranberry sauce, mixed pickles, pickled peaches and coleslaw. For the less well-off, pickles were a staple to relieve mundane fare. A housewife in Muncie, Indiana, speaking in 1890, described her winter diet:

Steak, roasts, macaroni, Irish potatoes, sweet potatoes, turnips, coleslaw, fried apples and stewed tomatoes, with Indian pudding, rice, cake, or pie for dessert. This was the winter repertoire of the average family that was not wealthy, and we swopped about from one combination to another using pickles and chow-chow to make the familiar starchy food relishing.[4]

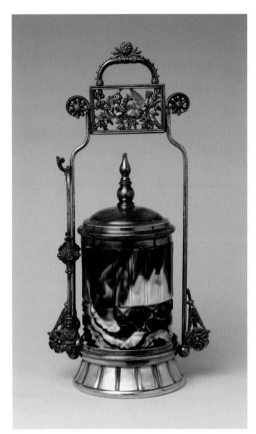

Pickle jar in pressed purple marble glass and metal, *c.* 1870–90, Challinor, Taylor & Co., Tarentum, Pennsylvania.

The American pickling tradition received a boost in the mid- to late nineteenth century with the arrival of Jewish immigrants, first from Germany and then from Eastern Europe and Russia, who introduced their own specialities: sauerkraut, salt beef and pickled tongue, *schmaltz* herrings in brine and 'Bismarks' – herrings pickled in vinegar; and what would become the titan of the deli counter, kosher dill pickles. The cucumbers were piled in wooden barrels and covered with brine prepared from koshering salt, flavoured with dill, spices and the defining ingredient that distinguishes a kosher dill pickle from an ordinary dill pickle – garlic. The cucumbers were left to ferment. A short time in brine produced 'half sours'; longer in brine, 'full sours'.

The Jewish predilection for pickled cucumbers was noteworthy: 'Probably no other people have so many kinds of "sours" as the Jews,' observed dietician Bertha Wood in her report *Foods of the Foreign-born in Relation to Health* (1922). She may have been right. *The Settlement Cookbook*, an amalgam of German Jewish and East European recipes published in 1901, gives eight recipes for pickled cucumbers. Many immigrants settled in the Lower East Side of Manhattan. Production of pickled vegetables, meat and fish soared to meet demand from a burgeoning population wanting the taste of home. Pushcarts laden with barrels of cucumbers in their cloudy tasty brines crowded the streets and alleys. Cucumber pickles could be purchased in quantity, singly or by the slice: a thick round sold for a penny piece and, placed in bread, was a popular lunch.

Wood voiced her disquiet on 'the limitations' of the Jewish diet and its wider implications:

> In the Jewish sections of our large cities there are storekeepers whose only goods are pickles. They have cabbages pickled whole, shredded, or chopped and rolled in leaves; peppers pickled; also string beans; cucumbers, sour, half sour, and salted; beets; and many kinds of meat and fish. This excessive use of pickled foods destroys the taste for milder flavors, causes irritation, and renders assimilation more difficult.

Wood's concerns over the consequences of pickle consumption echoed concerns that had surfaced earlier. Catharine Beecher, a prominent food reformer, observed in her *Letters to the People on Health and Happiness* (1856) that condiments 'stimulate the appetite to an unnatural degree'. Dr John Harvey Kellogg concurred. In *The Hygienic Cook Book* (1876) he listed the 'disease producing agents' that should be avoided: pickles, vinegar, spices and mustard head the hit list.

The predilection for pickles among American's newly arrived immigrants and the urban poor lead to moral consternation in other quarters. The socialist John Spargo, in his polemic *Bitter Cry of the Children* (1906), wrote of the woeful diet of many children living in poverty in America's major cities. Their diets, he observed, consisted for the most part of bread for breakfast and supper and pickles for lunch:

> For the children of the poor there seems to be some strange fascination about pickles. One lad of ten said that he always brought pickles with his three cents. 'I must have pickles' he said. It would seem that the chronic underfeeding creates a nervous craving for some kind of stimulant which the child finds in pickles. The adult resorts to whiskey very often for the same reason.

Concerns over the consequences of consuming pickles went unheeded. German-style delicatessens selling pickles and speciality foods flourished. They attracted a broad clientele and the East European tradition of pickled foods, above all those garlicky kosher dills, transcended cultural divides. Salt beef and kosher dills have become an essential part of the American food tradition: a symbol marking both ethnicity and integration. Kosher dills are made and consumed across America and among pickle aficionados they are regarded as the ultimate accompaniment to an overstuffed deli sandwich.

Until the mid-nineteenth century, pickling was for the most part a domestic activity. Commercial production was

Dill pickle spear and sweet pickle relish in a Chicago-style hot dog.

confined to foods that could be pickled and sold straight from barrels and to small-scale canners and bottlers who undertook the time-intensive bottling processes by hand, sealing each jar with cork and wire. In 1858 John L. Mason patented his glass jar with its self-sealing, airtight lid and transformed the process. For home preservers, the durable Mason jars were safe and easy to use. For manufacturers, the innovation of the zinc cap with its rubber gasket, coupled with faster methods for sterilizing the jar's contents, speeded up the bottling process. The timing couldn't have been better. The American Civil War led to a demand from the Union for canned foods to feed its army fighting in the distant South. By the end of the war, soldiers North and South had tried canned foods and commercial pickles. They liked the taste and they valued the convenience: demand soared. By the end of the century commercial pickles took the place of homemade and hundreds of small pickling and preserving companies were set up for business.

In 1869 Henry J. Heinz and L. Clarence Nobel went into business in Sharpsburg, Pennsylvania, to manufacture 'pure and superior' pickled horseradish, which they packaged in clear bottles to emphasize its quality. From a modest 1 acre field of horseradish, the company rapidly expanded its products to include pickled cucumbers and sauerkraut. In 1876 they launched the first commercial sweet pickles and tomato ketchup. By the turn of the century H. J. Heinz had become the largest manufacturer of pickled foods in the world. The company's strong association with cucumber pickles led to one of the greatest advertising coups in history: the creation of the Heinz 'pickle pin' – a branded, cucumber-shaped

Mrs Fidel Romero proudly exhibits her pickles and preserves, New Mexico, 1946. Mason jars with their special zinc caps made home pickling easy.

badge. At the Chicago World's Fair in 1893 more than one million pickle pins were handed out to entice visitors to the Heinz stand. The iconic pin is still produced; at the last count more than 100 million Heinz-branded pickle pins had been distributed.

A surfeit of cucumbers in the small agricultural town of Mount Olive, North Carolina, led to the creation of another pickle manufacturing giant. In 1926 Shikrey Baddour, a Lebanese immigrant, came up with the idea of buying the town's surplus cucumbers, pickling them and selling them on to other pickle companies to package and market. Buyers couldn't be found, but local businessmen, spotting the opportunity, established the Mt Olive Pickle Company to pack and sell the pre-brined pickles. By the 1950s the company led the way in research and development of cucumber pickling, working closely with the U.S. Department of Agriculture. The findings improved production methods throughout the industry. Mt Olive is now the best-selling cucumber pickle brand in the U.S.

From the early decades of the twentieth century, America pioneered new ways of manufacturing all manner of pickles that dispensed with traditional methods of preserving in brine and vinegar and used instead pasteurization and refrigeration. Many popular pickles in the U.S. are produced this way, including peppers, okra, watermelon rinds, mixed vegetables, cocktail onions and olives. But it is the cucumber, America's favourite pickle, that has seen the greatest changes from the brined original, notably sweetening the pickle liquor with sugar. The popularity of sweet and sour 'bread and butter pickles' is attributed to Illinois cucumber farmers Omar and Cora Fanning. Hard pressed for cash, the Fannings sliced up their undersized cucumbers and pickled them in a spiced vinegar and sugar syrup. Their recipe was not unique – a similar pickle appears in *The Settlement Cookbook* mentioned earlier – but the

The then world-famous high diver Beatrice Kyle posing with a pickle between acts at a benefit for the u.s. Army Relief Fund held at Fort Myer, Virginia, in 1924.

name was original and the couple trademarked 'Fanning's Bread and Butter Pickles' in 1923. Candied cucumber pickles, packed in heavily sweetened syrup, are a recent development. Along with the traditional fermented sour and half-sour kosher, dill and Polish pickles, pasteurized and refrigerated cucumber pickles come sugared, honeyed, peppered, garlicked, sweet/hot, spiced, sliced, diced, chopped, chipped and speared. There are at least 36 different styles of American pickled cucumbers to choose from.

6
From Asia to the Atlantic: Trade and Empire

The exotic pickles and relishes of South Asia have played a surprising and oft-forgotten role in the culinary canon of both Britain and America. It is a story of trade, empire and invention: of how cooks in the West enthusiastically assimilated the pickles, chutneys and *catchups* that arrived from the East. Piccalilli, with its strident mustard sauce, is testimony to British cooks' inventiveness in imitating Indian pickles; while the most popular of American condiments, tomato ketchup, owes its existence to a piquant sauce carried on the spice routes from Southeast Asia in the seventeenth century.

India

Early accounts of kingly feasts highlight the integral role pickles have played in Indian cuisine for centuries. In a manuscript from the eleventh century CE we read of pickles prepared with the spicy fruits of karira (*Capparis decidua*) and the crane berry (*Carissa carandas*). King Someshwara III, ruler of the Western Chaluka Kingdom in the twelfth century, includes the preparation of acidic relishes of yam, curds and fruit juices in his encyclopaedic *Mānasollāsa* (Refresher of the Mind), while the fictional King Nīlāpati in the poet Nemichandra's erotic novel *Lilāvati* (*c.* 1170) enjoys pickles of fruits, vegetables and roots, flavoured with camphor and presented on a lotus leaf.

The science of Ayurveda – 'life knowledge' – had established the value of pickles in the diet around 600 BCE. This decreed that a balanced meal comprised six basic *rasas* or tastes: *madhura*, sweet; *amla*, acid; *lavana*, saline; *katu*, pungent; *tikta*, bitter; and *kashaya*, astringent. The ancient Indians began meals with a sweet item, which included meat, and followed this with salt and sour; they ended with foods deemed pungent, bitter and astringent. Contemporary accounts describe relishes of mango, cucumber and tamarind preserved in vinegar or pickled in sour rice gruel. This custom has been

In Asia pickles are prepared using mustard oil or sesame oil in place of brine or vinegar. Here, chopped unripe mangos are combined with salt and spices before being covered in mustard oil and placed in the sun to ferment.

Mango pickle from Bihar made from chopped mangoes, white mustard, kalonji seeds, red chilli powder and rock salt.

maintained through the centuries. The seventeenth-century writer Annaji described a meal with 'a pickle of tender mangoes, the stalks of which had not even lost their fresh green colour; and vegetables delicately acid and salt'. In southern India, arranging food on a banana leaf, or in east India on a *thālī* – metal tray – allows the six tastes to be represented and savoured.

More than fifty pickles are described in a sixteenth-century Kannada manuscript known as the *Linga Purāna* of Gurulinga Dēsika (1594). There are pickles of lemons and limes, aubergines, chillies, onions and the most common, then as now, mango. Small unripe mangoes are pickled whole; large tender fruits are stoned and stuffed with fenugreek, mustard seed, asafoetida and chillies. Stuffed mangoes were some of the first Indian pickles to be exported to Britain, and were received with great excitement on the metropole's tables.

Other pickles in the *Linga Purāna* are prepared with mutton, wild boar, prawns and fish. These cooked meat pickles, common in the Punjab, and fish pickles, prepared more widely, may have been brought to the region by waves of Arab and Persian invaders from the eighth century onwards. The Hindi word for pickles – *āchār* – is commonly ascribed as Persian in origin. The method of making pickles set down at this time has changed little. Here we find instructions for pickling in mustard or sesame oil rather than conventional brine or vinegar, a practice that is unique to India, Pakistan and Bangladesh. Mustard oil is used more in the north and east and sesame oil in the south and west. To complete the pickling process the filled jars are placed in the sun to mature, adhering to the ritual category of 'cooking without fire', using instead the fierce heat of the sun to destroy any microbes or moulds and prevent spoilage.

While pickles are for long keeping, another traditional relish, *chatni* – chutney – is for more immediate consumption and is often freshly made. Prepared from a legion of fruits, vegetables, seeds and nuts, *chatni* comes chopped like a relish or pounded to a paste; it may be herbed, spiced, sweet, sour, hot or mild, fresh or cooked. Chutneys of sour cherries and lotus stems are a speciality of Kashmir in the north; plums, figs, apricots and apple of Bengal in the east. Sweet mango is popular in the west, coconut in the south, and chutneys of fish or prawn are common along India's southwestern tip. Northeast India has a tradition of aged chutneys, prepared from fermented cooked soybean or fermented fish mixed with salt and chillies, which take the place of pickles. The cultural as well as culinary importance of *chatni* was traditionally marked by Indian Muslims during Muharram, the start of the Islamic year. As part of the festivities, the comic character of Chutnee Shah appeared. He was instantly recognizable by

Sweet lemon pickle, with its combination of sweet, hot and sour flavours, is popular in southern India.

the small mortar tied to his loins and a pestle carried in his hand. Writing in 1863, Jaffur Shurreef provides an account of the spectacle:

> Having put into the mortar a little green ginger, garlic, tamarind, chillies, sweetmeats, *majoon*, *bhung*, in short anything eatable, he pounds them, singing, 'I am making *qazee's chutnee*!', 'I am making *kotioal's chutnee*!', 'I am making *soobulidar's chutnee*!', 'Most delicious *chutnee*!', 'Bravo, *chutnee*!' . . . Occasionally both men and women among the spectators beg some of it; for being composed of a variety of eatables it has at the time a very agreeable taste; but when *majoon* or *bhung* is mixed with it, the young and old people, not accustomed to the use of inebriating substances, are so much affected by it, that some lie insensible for hours, while others become incoherent in their speech.[1]

India's pickles and chutneys were introduced to Britain from the end of the seventeenth century. Their exotic ingredients and arresting flavours invigorated and transformed the British kitchen and travelled on to America, inspiring in both countries a panoply of piquant pickles, relishes and condiments which continue to be made today.

Britain

The English were great exponents of pickling. The word 'pickle' first appears in the English language around 1400, derived from the Dutch *pēkel*. At first it referred to a spicy sauce served with meat, but it soon came to mean brine or vinegar in which food was preserved. The seventeenth century marked the high point of vinegar pickles in Britain. This was a time of experimentation and innovation fired by developments at home and abroad. The expansion of the kitchen garden, begun in the late sixteenth century, gave an abundance of produce to preserve, while trade with India brought exotic pickles to the table, first to taste and then to emulate. Pickles were invaluable to the cook: they were used in winter salads, stirred into hashes and meat fricassees to give piquancy and, as now, appreciated as relishes.

Cookbooks of the period devote chapters to pickling and to making vinegars from sour wine or ale, which was known as alegar. The list of herbs and vegetables destined for the pickling crock was almost endless: artichokes, asparagus, cucumbers, peas, French beans, purslane, mushrooms, lettuce, succory, samphire, beetroots, burdock roots, parsnips, white and red cabbages and cauliflower. Some vegetables were plunged straight into vinegar pickle, others spent a short time in brine, which improved their flavour. Orchards and glasshouses offered similar bounty. Stone and soft fruits, formerly conserved in sugar syrup, were deemed ripe for vinegar pickling. Lemons, which for a century or more had been preserved whole in brine, were prepared in spiced or sugared vinegar. Cowslips and clove gillyflowers (pinks) were pickled in wine vinegar and sugar, rose hips in alegar and sugar. One pickle, often regarded as quintessentially British, but surprisingly absent from early modern cookbooks, is pickled eggs. Isabella Beeton in *The Book of Household Management* (1861) puts matters right. She pickles hard-boiled eggs in vinegar with black pepper, ginger and allspice, advising her readers: 'A store of pickled eggs will be found very useful and ornamental in serving with many first and second course dishes.'

Pickled onions, with bread and cheese, are an essential part of a British ploughman's lunch.

Pickled eggs, traditionally served in Britain's pubs and fish and chip shops, are enjoyed as a snack, often washed down with beer or cider.

Exotic Indian pickles arrived in the second half of the seventeenth century. Bamboo shoots were one curiosity, but mangoes, pungent with mustard seeds and spices, attracted the greatest excitement: these curious fruits arrested the eye and tantalized the tastebuds. English cooks set to work to reproduce these South Asian novelties. Tender elder shoots were bottled in vinegar with fresh ginger and spices as 'imitation' or 'English' bamboo, while whole pickled 'mangoes' were fashioned from cucumbers, melons and peaches. John Evelyn in *Acetaria: A Discourse of Sallets* (1699) prepared 'Mango of Cucumbers'. He selects large cucumbers, carefully slits them, scoops out the seeds, and puts in their place garlic or roccombo seeds (wild onion). The cucumbers are stuffed into a jar and boiled in spiced vinegar brine, before being finished with 'a good spoonful of the best mustard'. What began as a novelty had lasting appeal. Maria Rundell in *A New System of Cookery* (1806) prepared 'Melon Mangoes' in much the same way, a fashion that travelled to North America. The British taste for Indian pickles continues unabated: mango pickles, aubergine pickles and mouth-puckering lime pickles are still imported from India.

The creation of piccalilli – crunchy vegetables in a vinegar-mustard liquor – was the crowning and lasting glory of British enthusiasm for imitating Indian pickles. Lady Anne Blencowe, in her personal receipt book of 1694, provides the first known recipe for 'Pickle Lila, an Indian Pickle'. A large quantity of garlic and fresh ginger, cabbages, cauliflowers, celery, French beans, asparagus and peppers are salted and dried in the sun, then pickled in vinegar and brine with bruised mustard seed and fine turmeric. The preparation was sufficiently unusual to appear authentic and the distinctive 'Indian Pickle' became an enduring standard in Britain's pickle repertoire. The London critic Eneas Dallas, in *Kettner's Book of the Table* (1877), noted the change in British tastes: 'The best mixed pickles . . . are now made with a woe-begone compound called Piccalilli.' There were others besides. Dallas continued: 'East India pickles – strange irrecognisable compounds confused with curry, an amazing jumble of hot, sweet, sour, and bitter things – have come into fashion.'

Varieties of beetroot for pickling. The catalogue notes: 'Vinegar in which Beets have been pickled is often used to pickle hard-boiled eggs, as it gives them a beautiful colour and pleasant flavour.' From John Lewis Childs's spring catalogue for 1903.

The nineteenth century witnessed the rise in commercial pickling and a decline in the variety of pickles. London was the epicentre of the pickle industry: 'It is remarkable how that even country people must buy London pickles,' observes the *Grocer's Manual* in 1896. Onions and cucumbers were grown close to the capital, while France, the Netherlands and even America cultivated gherkins, cucumbers, onions and cauliflowers and shipped them in brine to meet Britain's insatiable appetite for mixed pickles, pickled cucumbers and onions and piccalilli. The quality of factory-made pickles was often found wanting, prepared with low-grade vegetables, commercial acetic acid and water, and 'coloured to fancy'. Yet there had been far worse. Cucumbers, French beans, peppers and samphire lost their colour when pickled. One way to avoid an unappetizing grey pickle was to repeatedly pour boiling vinegar over the vegetables. A quicker method, used by commercial pickle-makers, was to add copper, either by steeping or boiling the vegetables in vinegar in a copper pot, or by adding 'bluestone' (sulphate of copper). The copper reacted with the vinegar and rendered the vegetables a 'fine lively green'. There was a high price to pay for aesthetics – verdigris poisoning. The chemist Frederick Accum, in *A Treatise on Adulterations of Food and Culinary Poisons* (1820), included this exposé:

> Dr Percival has given an account of 'a young lady who amused herself, while her hair was dressing, with eating samphire pickles impregnated with copper. She soon complained of pain in the stomach; and, in five days, vomiting commenced, which was incessant for two days. After this, her stomach became prodigiously distended; and, in nine days after eating the pickle, death relieved her from her suffering.'

It was another thirty years before the practice was banned.

Pickling not only provided relishes for the table, but more substantial foods such as pickled pork, salt beef and pickled fish. William Ellis, writing in *The Country Housewife's Companion* (1750), cannot be more emphatic about the gastronomic merits of pork pickled in salt brine: 'the flesh of a well-chosen hog', he declares, eats 'tender and luscious'. Pickled beef, or salt beef as it was known in London, was prepared in a similar manner. The pickle, with its combination of coarse salt, saltpetre (curing salt), soft brown sugar, bay leaves, juniper berries and spices, gave the beef its soft texture and delicate flavour. Salt beef became the linchpin of the Jewish delicatessen trade in London and New York in the early twentieth century, a tradition which continues.

Somewhat earlier, Hannah Glasse in *The Art of Cookery* (1758 edition) included a recipe for raw beef salted and barrelled in vinegar, which 'will keep a Year good in the Pickle, and with care, will go to the East-Indies'. Pickled foods were an essential part of a ship's provisions. The art of pickling flesh was occasionally called into service for other means. In 1610 the English naval commander Admiral Sir George Somers died in Barbados, reportedly 'of a surfeit of eating a pig'. His heart was buried there, but his body was returned to his birthplace, the harbour town of Lyme Regis, pickled in a barrel.

Sir Hugh Platt in *Delightes for the Ladies* (1602) was one of the first to share the culinary 'secret' of pickling (or sousing) cooked meat, giving instructions for roast beef in wine-vinegar, which, he promised, will keep a long time 'sweete and wholesome'. The pickled meats, thinly sliced and served with more vinegar, were valued as side dishes to pep up the tastebuds, and just like vegetable pickles, they were prepared as 'grand salads'. Pickles of a singular kind were made from small birds. Eliza Smith, in *The Compleat Housewife* (1727), instructed readers to boil sparrows and put them in a strong pickle of Rhenish wine and white wine vinegar, 'high with salt', seasoned with aromatics and spices. The sparrows stay in their souse for some time. Smith advised that 'when the bones are dissolved they are fit to eat; put them in china-saucers, and mix with your Pickles.'

Pickled fish and shellfish were commonplace in Britain until the advent of the railways, which enabled fresh fish to be transported quickly. Herrings, pilchards, sprats and smelts – the last two used in place of imported anchovies – were barrelled in brine. Oysters, cockles, mussels and winkles were stewed in their juices with vinegar and spices, while shrimps were pickled in alegar (strong ale vinegar) and salt. Alegar was revealed as the secret pickling medium for the famous 'New-castle salmon', sent to London by the barrelful. The salmon, cooked with plenty of salt in beer and water, then pickled in

alegar and spices, lasted a year and was a staple food of the poor until the early nineteenth century. The upper classes preferred to fry fresh fish in oil and place it in white wine vinegar. Sir Hugh Platt advised his readers, 'you may keep it for the use of your table any reasonable time.' This method was known to the Romans as well as to the Arabs, who introduced it to Spain. How the method came to Britain, or whether it was arrived at independently, is not clear. Writing much later, Hannah Glasse in *The Art of Cookery Made Plain and Easy* (1747) employed the same method for mackerel, which she called 'Caveach'. Pickled fish served well as an appetizer, condiment or side dish: attributes that have kept both soused herrings and pickled rollmops on the menu.

The medieval court cookbook of Richard II provides the earliest English recipe for chutney. A casual reader of *The Forme of Cury* (1390) may be forgiven for passing it by: it appears under the unpromising title of 'compost'. To prepare the chutney the king's master cooks took white turnips, parsnips, radishes and pears, cut them into chunks and boiled them. Once cold, they added salt, vinegar, spices and saffron and let the mixture stand overnight. The following day they stirred in Greek wine and honey, Lombardy mustard, raisins, currants, walnuts, sweet spices and seeds of anise and fennel. The compost was stored in an earthenware pot and used as required. This elaborate concoction can be traced back to ancient Rome and the simple recipe given by Apicius for turnips preserved in honey and vinegar, mentioned earlier.

The British enthusiasm for chutney came much later, ignited by the taste of Indian relishes encountered early in the history of colonial rule. The Indian elite served pickles and *chatni* at breakfast and dinner to accompany curries, kebabs, fried fish and fowl and to liven up plain rice and dal. The appeal of these pungently spiced pastes and side dishes is captured in the words of F. Ward in *India and the Hindoos* (1850): 'the meal . . . is rendered all the more delicious by pickles, chitneys, and other condiments that tempt the appetite of a Hindoo epicure.' The British were keen to replicate these exciting flavours, and Anglo-Indian chutney and pickle recipes, combining exotic ingredients with the British penchant for vinegar, appear in colonial household manuals for the memsahib and her cook. Indian chutneys – the term being anglicized from the Hindi *chatni* – began to be exported to

Britain towards the end of the nineteenth century. Production was centred in the East India Company's settlements of Bombay, Madras and Calcutta. For the most part these Anglo-Indian chutneys took their cue from fruit-based, cooked *chatni*, often with mango as their main constituent and with an emphasis on sweetness rather than the sweet, sour and hot of the original relish.

Law's Grocer's Manual of 1896 includes entries for some of the best-known imported Indian chutneys, among them Bengal, Calcutta Howrah, Madras, Cashmere, Lucknow and Tirhoot; and, exploiting associations with the British Raj, Colonel Skinner's and Major Grey's. The spicy hot Tirhoot, prepared from sweetened sliced fruits, was legendary and, as *Law's* notes, was 'considered by many to be the best of all'. Major Grey's Chutney continues, in name at least, to be made by various companies in the UK, U.S. and in India, and inspired the comic verse by John F. Mackay:

> All things chickeney and mutt'ny
> Taste better far when served with chutney
> This is the mystery eternal:
> Why didn't Major Grey make colonel?

The original recipe is said to have come from an officer in the Bengal Lancers. Either he or his Bengali cook created the mild chutney, combining typical *chatni* ingredients: mangoes, raisins, garlic, chillies, vinegar, lime and tamarind juice, salt, sugar and spices. Major Grey subsequently sold his recipe to the British condiment manufacturer Crosse & Blackwell, which had a presence in India.

Chutneys inspired by Indian imports were also made in Britain, although as *Law's* observes: 'all imitations are much inferior in aroma to the genuine, made from the widely-famed

Major Grey's Chutney was created in India in the late 19th century, expressly for the British market, and was one of many produced and exported at this time.

gardens of the East.' These British chutneys used orchard fruits in place of mango and generous quantities of sugar. Eliza Acton in *Modern Cookery* (1845) attributed her recipe for 'Chatney Sauce' to Bengal. It is prepared from sour or crab apples, pounded with raisins, brown sugar, salt, ginger, cayenne pepper and vinegar to the consistency of thick cream and then bottled. A Bengali cook may not have recognized the recipe and Acton is uncertain of its merits. She advised

The recipe for Lea & Perrins's 'Original and Genuine Worcester Sauce' reputedly came from Bengal and includes tamarind pickled in vinegar and anchovies pickled in brine. It was found on all the best tables in the mid-1800s. Advertising claims that the condiment was used by the royal family heightened its social acceptability and popularity.

that the sauce will keep better on being exposed to gentle heat for a week or two, either by the side of the fire or in full sun. The ingredients are similar to those used for apple chutney made today, although now the mixture is boiled and bottled, which produces a sweet-and-sour chutney jam.

Chutneys, suitably anglicized, were quickly assimilated into British culinary culture and their imperial lineage forgotten. Apple chutney is seen as a traditional countryside preserve. Other commercial products have been created in a chutney style. One of the best known is Branston Pickle, a spiced vegetable mixture in a tangy brown sauce, first made in the Staffordshire village of Branston in 1922. Spicy brown bottled table sauces such as HP, which are based on the astringent Indian fruit tamarind and various spices, also belong to the Indian tradition. Lea & Perrins 'Original and Genuine

Worcester Sauce', created in 1835 by Worcester chemists John Wheeley Lea and William Henry Perrins, was from a recipe belonging to Lord Sandys which he had reputedly acquired in Bengal. The mixture, which includes tamarind and vegetables pickled in vinegar, and anchovies pickled in brine, was deemed inedible and was set aside. Rediscovering the barrels many months later, it was found that the sauce had matured and mellowed. Lea and Perrins began to make the fermented sauce from their chemist's shop in 1837. Today, the ingredients which comprise Worcestershire sauce are left for eighteen months before being blended and bottled.

The Atlantic Pickle: Ketchup

Pickled vegetables gave rise to another form of relish – ketchup. The story of ketchup begins in late seventeenth-century Britain and reaches its zenith in nineteenth-century America, the nomenclature and ingredients evolving on the journey from the Old World to the New. British cooks discovered that the rich, dark liquor created from pickling mushrooms made a tasty condiment in its own right and some took to bottling it. This development coincided with the introduction of an alluring piquant sauce called catchup, which came via the spice trade from Southeast Asia, and is first recorded in English in 1699, where it is simply described as a 'high East-India Sauce'.[2]

How catchup acquired its name is not known. Likewise, the ingredients of this Eastern catchup were, and remain, a mystery. It may have been a type of soy sauce, a fish and brine pickle similar to modern Thai fish sauce, or not one but a variety of similar products. The desire to replicate these salty, nuanced flavours from the East encouraged experimentation in the kitchen, spurred by the realization that the taste of mushroom pickle-liquor bore a similarity to the import. The earliest recipe for 'English Katchop' appears in Eliza Smith's *Compleat Housewife* (1727). She takes anchovies, shallots, white wine and vinegar, horseradish, lemon peel and spices. The mixture is boiled, bottled and left for a week, being shaken daily. The recipe caught the eye of other cookery writers and it appears in numerous cookbooks of the period.

Through the course of the eighteenth and early nineteenth century, ever more concentrated catchups (or catsups) were devised from pickling familiar foods – first mushrooms, quickly followed by green walnuts, elderberries, cucumbers, cockles, mussels and oysters. To create the richly flavoured liquor, the brine or vinegar pickle was fortified with strong ale, red wine, anchovies, garlic, horseradish, sherry or port. At the end of the process the pickle was strained, the flavouring ingredients discarded and the resulting liquor reduced by boiling. These savoury catchups were the height of fashion – the condiment of choice to add relish and savour to ordinary foods. The character John Willet, proprietor of the Maypole Inn in Charles Dickens's novel *Barnaby Rudge* (1841), set in London in 1780, hungrily instructs his cook to bring him 'lamb chops (breaded, with plenty of ketchup)'.

The commercial manufacture of ketchups gave rise to a range of proprietary ketchups and sauces which used them as a basis. Among them were Camp, prepared from anchovies, beer and sherry; Marine, with added shallots; Pontac, from elderberries; Windermere, from mushrooms and horseradish; Wolfram, beer with anchovies and mushrooms; and Quin and Harvey, both based on mushroom ketchup. Along with their piquant pickle flavours, the keeping qualities of ketchups, just as with the pickles that had given rise to them, were part of their appeal. Their longevity became legendary.

Hannah Glasse in *The Art of Cookery* (1747) included ketchup prepared from pickling mushrooms and anchovies, which she confidently titled, 'Catchup to keep twenty Years'.

One catchup to appear late on the culinary scene, but which today is almost synonymous with the word ketchup, was tomato. It was in America that tomato catchup came into its own. America acquired its liking of catchups from Britain. English cookbooks were widely available, and homemade catchups and later imported bottled sauces proved just as popular in the New World as in the Old. Ultimately, the variety of North American ketchups, prepared from every conceivable variety of fruit, far exceeded those of Britain. And it was here, in the opening decades of the nineteenth century, that the potential of the tomato was realized.

In 1804 James Mease, a prominent Philadelphia scientist, observed that 'Love Apples' made 'a fine catsup'; six years later he was the first to publish a recipe. He took tomatoes, sliced them thinly, sprinkled them with salt and left them overnight. The next day they were simmered, spiced with mace and allspice, and the cooked pulp bottled with a hint of shallot and glug of brandy.[3] Mease's recipe, which is representative of others from this time, bore little resemblance to conventional catchups. Notably, the product which resulted was not a pickle liquor but a thick sauce. Despite this anomaly, the fashionable, and highly marketable, name of catsup, catchup or ketchup – which had also entered the vocabulary – stuck fast. By 1830 commercial production of tomato ketchup was underway.

Early tomato ketchup recipes were quickly improved upon. Flavourings were generous and included onions, shallots, garlic, peppers, horseradish and anchovies, along with spices such as mustard, black pepper, cayenne pepper, allspice, cloves and ginger. Increasingly, vinegar was added as a preservative. These original tomato ketchups were spicy and tart. There was one defining ingredient yet to be added to the cooking pot – sugar. The inclusion of brown sugar became prevalent in the latter half of the nineteenth century, mirroring the American taste for sweet foods. The move was compounded by an upsurge in industrial production following the American Civil War and a marked decline in making ketchup in the home.

Hundreds of companies took to making tomato ketchup across the u.s., among them H. J. Heinz, which launched its tomato ketchup in 1876 using, as producers did at the time, home-style recipes. As the twentieth century dawned Heinz was set to become the world's largest producer of tomato ketchup. By 1907 the company was producing over 12 million bottles per annum and shipping wooden casks of ketchup across the globe: to Britain, mainland Europe, South Africa, South America, Australia, New Zealand, and even to China and Japan, the world's most prodigious producers and consumers of pickles. The sweet and sour taste of commercial tomato ketchups, coupled with their bright colour and dense consistency, appealed to American consumers. Traditional recipes were changed and 'improved'. Above all, the amount of sugar and vinegar increased substantially through the decades to create the archetypal modern American ketchup, with its sweet tomato taste and vinegar tang.

The American South gave rise to another international pickle sauce, Tabasco. Edmund McIlhenny began making his fiery sauce from hot chilli peppers on Avery Island in Louisiana in the late 1860s, in a desire to pep up the bland and monotonous diet of the Reconstruction-era South. He selected the reddest peppers from the plants he had grown, crushed them, and mixed them with Avery Island salt, leaving them to ferment in crockery jars and barrels for thirty days.

Advertisement for Heinz tomato ketchup, USA, 1939.

Tabasco Pepper
Sauce, Victorian
trade card,
c. 1900.

He added French wine vinegar and left them for a further
thirty days or more. The strained sauce was transferred to
small bottles, corked and sealed with wax. McIlhenny's hot
sauce proved so popular with family and friends that he gave
up his banking career and started commercial production in
1868, securing a patent two years later. Tabasco is still made
on Avery Island by the fifth generation of the McIlhenny
family. The method has changed little, except it takes rather
more time: the salted chilli peppers now spend up to three
years ageing in white oak barrels. As with many pickles, the
pungent, piquant flavour has universal appeal: today, Tabasco
Sauce is labelled in 22 languages and dispatched to more than
180 countries.[4]

7
Pickles Today

Pickles are big business. In 2015 the global pickle market was valued at more than $11 billion. Japan accounts for more than one-quarter of the market, closely followed by the United States. Together, they comprise just under half of the world's commercial pickle market by value, with Mexico, Brazil and Germany, each with significantly smaller markets, making up the top five.

Demand for pickles in recent times has been driven by their growing popularity as a relish to accompany fast foods, sandwiches, hotdogs, hamburgers and pizzas; and, at the other end of the spectrum, by the associated health benefits of consuming fermented pickles. Naturally fermented pickles continue to be an essential part of culinary culture across the world, including countries such as China, Korea, India and Russia, where home pickling is common, but also in the developed commercial markets of Japan and Germany. The United States is the exception. Here, non-fermented pasteurized and acidified pickles dominate sales, and to meet demand most products are imported. Americans consume over 4 kg (8–9 lb) of pickles per person each year, primarily cucumbers and peppers: more than fifteen varieties of pepper are offered 'pickled'. The U.S. demand for fermented cucumber pickles comes primarily from the catering industry, which requires traditional dill pickles for hamburgers.

Modern Pickles

America has been at the forefront of pickle commercialization and innovation – above all, Americans dispensed with the traditional practice of fermentation and devised novel ways to manufacture pickles by using processes that take a fraction of the time. In the early twentieth century, the Californians pioneered the development of the unfermented canned olive. This was a double invention: not only does the method dispense with fermentation, it turns unripe green olives into 'ripe' black olives. The process begins in the conventional manner: green olives are immersed in sodium hydroxide to break down the bitter glucoside oleuropein,

Pickle packaging has undergone a small revolution in the last decade. Single-serve pickle packs and stand-up pouches offer added convenience, while the classic glass pickle jar has been replicated in unbreakable PET plastic which is lighter and saves on transport costs.

Pickle fermentation vats, North Carolina. The scale of commercial pickle production has environmental consequences because of the amount of salt in the spent brine. Companies are looking at various ways of reducing the salt in waste water, including recycling the brine.

which otherwise renders them inedible. Then, the alchemy: dissolved oxygen and a solution of iron salts are bubbled through the vats; these react with the phenolic compounds in the olive's skin turning it from green to black. The 'black' olives are canned in brine and sterilized. These unfermented, cooked olives, with their slippery texture and bland, soapy flavour, appear on pizzas the world over.

The twentieth century also heralded 'fresh pack' pickles. These are prepared from raw fresh fruit and vegetables which, immediately after picking, are bottled in brine or other liquor, often a mixture of vinegar and sugar syrup. To compensate for their lack of flavour, extra salt, sugar and spices are added. The jars are vacuum sealed and pasteurized to improve their shelf-life. An alternative method, known as acidified or refrigerated pickles, involves pickling fresh vegetables in brine with vinegar or acetic acid, salt and flavourings, then chilling

The growing demand for natural foods and interest in the health benefits of pickles has led to a proliferation of small producers offering traditionally fermented products.

immediately. The vegetables have a fresh taste and crispness but do not keep. A non-fermented form of sauerkraut is also industrially produced, although it lacks the distinctive taste and health benefits of traditional sauerkraut. The vinegared, mild-flavoured cabbage is popular in the United States as a relish for hotdogs and sandwiches.

In the twenty-first century, new pickle lines have appeared to meet consumer demand for products with less sugar or salt and for additive-free, non-genetically modified (non-GMO) and organic pickles. In 2001 Mt Olive, one of America's largest pickle manufacturers, launched its 'No Sugar Added' pickle range, using artificial sweetener in its place. Concern over the high salt content of pickles has led to a new method for pickling cucumbers that replaces conventional sodium chloride (common salt) with calcium chloride (another form of salt). Calcium chloride not only retains the crispness of the cucumbers and speeds up fermentation, but has an extremely salty taste, meaning less is required to flavour the pickles. The process has an added environmental benefit: calcium chloride is less polluting than sodium chloride. To minimize their environmental impact, pickling plants must recycle the spent brine or limit the amount of salt discharged into waste water. Calcium chloride waste can be used as a soil enhancer.

Established players such as Del Monte lead the field in organic and non-GMO pickles, which are marketed as 'natural' and 'simple'; sugar may be used in place of high-fructose corn syrup, turmeric instead of artificial yellow colourants and sea salt rather than rock salt. The growing trend for

Pickle juice has become a popular sports aid in the U.S., sold as drinks and frozen as ice pops. Bob's Pickle Pops are marketed as a muscle pick-me-up for athletes.

natural foods has encouraged artisan pickle producers to enter the u.s. market, offering authentic brined and fermented pickles and sporting brand names such as Real Pickles, Jeff's Naturals and Olive My Pickle, which capitalize on the wholesome, natural association. Since 2000 pickle juice drinks have appeared, marketed as sports aids. Their introduction is attributed to the now legendary 'pickle juice game' in the National Football League of September that year when the Philadelphia Eagles beat the Dallas Cowboys 41–14, in temperatures that topped 40°C (104°F). The Eagles' vigour was attributed to the pickle juice they drank to combat the heat and stave off cramp. A further novel invention, Bob's Pickle Pops, made from the frozen pulp and brine of pickled cucumbers, and heralded as the healthy alternative to ice cream, was created by Texan John Howard and launched in 2008.

The Pickleback

According to popular folklore, the term 'pickleback' – the act of accompanying bourbon with a shot of pickle brine – was coined by bartender Reggie Cunningham of Bushwick Country Club, Brooklyn, in 2006. One evening, Cunningham was introduced to the pairing by a customer from the southern United States, from where it is thought to have originated. The combination of pickles and alcohol is common elsewhere: pickles with vodka in Russia and pickles with tequila in Mexico, for example. Through the course of that evening Cunningham downed, he says, a dozen shots of Old Crow bourbon chased by brine from a jar of McClure's Spicy Dills. The brine neutralized the burn and taste of the bourbon to leave a savoury tang. Cunningham awoke without a hangover and was convinced of the combination – the pickleback was added to the Club's drinks menu. From Brooklyn, the pickleback, with its catchy name, swiftly spread to bars across New York, San Francisco and London.

The pickleback evolved as it travelled. Bartenders offer their own combinations and prepare their own speciality brines; some provide a whole dill pickle as an accompaniment. New York's Crocodile Lounge offers the Dirty Sanchez – Espolon tequila with jalapeño pickle juice – and Boulton and Watt on 5th Avenue sell the Pick your Pickleback (Tullamore Dew Irish Whiskey paired with a shot of traditional brine, pickled beet juice or pineapple, mint and habanero pickle). In London, Pitt Cue, which introduced the pickleback to the UK in 2011, serves classic American bourbon with its own herbed and spiced brine used for pickling cucumbers for the restaurant. The pickleback has also reached Paraguay, where it has taken on a tropical twist – pickle brine partners the local rum.

Pickles and Health

The health benefits associated with the consumption of lacto-fermented pickles have been well documented. Naturally fermented pickles are a rich source of beneficial probiotic microbes and essential vitamins and minerals. Analysis of Korea's traditional pickled cabbage, kimchi, has revealed that 1 g contains around 800 million bacteria which help maintain a healthy gut, aid digestion and promote good health more broadly. Nutritional studies of kimchi and sauerkraut, first associated with preventing scurvy in the eighteenth century, have shown that fermentation preserves the vitamins found in fresh cabbage, including vitamins A, B, C and K.[1] Medical research suggests that this power pack of vitamins, trace elements, antioxidants and active plant compounds called glucosinolates could possess both anti-ageing and anti-cancer properties. A 2005 study among U.S. Polish migrants found that a high intake of sauerkraut correlates with a reduced risk of breast cancer in women.[2] Researchers in Korea have identified that cabbage kimchi has anti-ageing, anti-mutagenic, anti-cancer and anti-metastatic properties, as well as enhancing the body's natural immune system. The consumption of kimchi is claimed to have protected the South Korean population from the SARS (severe acute respiratory syndrome) pandemic in Asia in 2003.[3]

However, other evidence suggests there can be too much of a good thing. Studies across Asia, including in China and southern India, have linked high levels of pickle consumption with higher risk of cancers of the throat and stomach. A recent study in Singapore, where salt-fermented vegetables are widely consumed, found that those who consumed vegetables pickled in salt brine at least once a week were four times more likely to develop nasopharyngeal cancer than those who never or rarely ate them. The scientists attribute a possible cause to carcinogenic compounds found in salted vegetables, although little is known about these.[4] More commonly, especially in the West, health concerns are directed at the salt content of pickles: consuming too much salt can cause high blood pressure and heart disease.

Yet salt also fulfils a vital function in the body: it helps regulate the body's fluids, blood pH levels, nerve impulses and muscle function. And this is how pickle brine comes into its own as a cure for hangovers: it is a natural source of sodium, magnesium and potassium, and helps to restore the body's electrolyte and fluid levels. The Germans go a step further and serve *Rollmöpse*, pickled herrings, as part of the *Katerfrühstück* – hangover breakfast. Drinking pickle juice also helps prevent muscle cramp in athletes, but in a very different way. Research by a team at North Dakota State University suggests that the effect is neurological. Within 85 seconds of downing a small quantity of pickle juice strained from a jar of cucumbers pickled in vinegar, muscle cramps ceased. It seems that the pickle juice (possibly because of the vinegar) triggers a nerve reaction that revokes the misfiring of alpha motor neurons in the cramping muscle.[5]

Vinegar pickle liquor has been shown to have specific benefits for those with type 2 diabetes who need to control their blood sugar levels. Taken before a meal, vinegar pickle juice reduces blood sugar spikes, which occur after consuming carbohydrate-heavy foods. While vinegar itself is known to have this effect, its taste and harshness mean drinking it regularly is impractical; however, researchers at Arizona State University suggest that for people who are pre-diabetic or have developed type 2 diabetes, including foods pickled in vinegar in their diet may help them manage their condition.[6]

The Future

This century, the commercial production of pickles is set to grow as home pickling continues to decline, owing to urbanization or rising affluence. This trend is already underway in South Korea as people move from the countryside into towns. India, Russia and Brazil may see a similar pattern. In the quest to further improve fermentation methods, scientists are exploring the molecular ecology of vegetable fermentation and the mathematical modelling of bacterial growth and competition. On the environmental agenda is the use of closed-tank technology to reduce salt waste and improving the quality of recycled pickle brine by removing enzymes that soften foods.

Research, still in its infancy, is intended to hone the flavour of pickles. Studies on the physiology and chemistry of sour taste, which is surprisingly little understood, may ultimately enable manufacturers to heighten a consumer's sensory perception and pleasure of eating pickles.

Fermented pickles make a significant contribution to the diets and well-being of millions of people. In recent decades, as the processes of fermentation have become better understood, attention has turned to the potential of fermented foods and pickles to alleviate food shortages. This work has two dimensions: first, in developing countries where pickles are a staple food, improving methods to enhance their quality; and second, exploring how pickling can be introduced and adapted to regions where the practice is underutilized or unknown. The advantage of fermented pickles is that they are a natural, low-technology and low-energy means of extending the shelf-life of perishable foods, without the need for refrigeration. In this way, fermented pickles could be just one practical contribution to meeting the growing global demand for food.

Recipes

Historical Recipes

Turnip and Mustard Greens

From Jia Sixie, *Qi min yao shu* (Important Arts for the People's Welfare, 544 CE)

After soaking for three days [in very salty water], remove the vegetables. Grind panicum millet and use the flour to make a congee [gruel]. Decant the thin decoction. Take wheat *ferment (mai hun)*,* grind it and sift the powder through a silk screen. Spread a layer of vegetables [in a jar], sprinkle on lightly a coating of ferment powder, and then cover it with the hot thin congee. Repeat this process until the jar is full. When forming a layer, the bundles of vegetables should be placed side by side in such a way that the head of one is next to the tail of the other, and so on. The original salt solution is then poured into the jar [before it is sealed]. The pickle will have a yellow colour and a pleasant flavour.

*Mould ferments were prepared from cakes of cooked wheat or rice left to develop a powdery covering of yellow mould, typically *Aspergillus* and *Rhizopus*.

Mālih bi-Khall wa-Kahardal (Salted Fish with Vinegar and Mustard)

From al-Baghdādī, *Kitāb al-Tabīkh* (Book of Recipes), trans. Charles Perry as *A Baghdad Cookery Book* (Totnes, 2005)

Fry it [salted fish] in sesame oil . . . and take it out of the pan and leave it in vinegar in which you have put finely pounded mustard seed and a little finely powdered coriander. Colour the vinegar with a little saffron.

Grape Pickle

From Turabi Efendi, *A Turkish Cookery Book, A Collection of Receipts* (London, 1865)

Procure ten or twelve pounds of either black or white grapes, pick out the best bunches, and squeeze the juice from the bruised and small ones, pass it through a sieve into a stew pan, free from smell, and set it to boil for a few minutes; then wash the bunches you have selected, and lay two or three of them on the bottom of a stone jar; then sprinkle some mustard seeds over, then grapes, again mustard seeds over; then grapes, and continue so till the whole of the grapes are laid; then pour the boiled grape-juice over, cover the jar air-tight, and let it remain for thirty or forty days before using. They will keep for a long time, and are very refreshing on account of their agreeable acidity.

Sweet Pickles

From Mrs Simon (Lizzie) Kandor, *The 'Settlement' Cook Book* (Milwaukee, WI, 1901)

4 quarts (4.5 l) tiny cucumbers
1½ cups (300 g) salt to 2 quarts (2 l) water
1 gallon (3.7 l) vinegar
2 cups (340 g) brown sugar
4 whole red peppers

2 sticks cinnamon, broken
2 tbsp allspice, whole
2 tbsp cloves, heads removed
2 tbsp mustard seeds
¼ cup (40 g) horseradish root, diced

Lay cucumbers in the salt water over night and drain. Let vinegar, peppers, sugar and whole spices come to a boil, throw in the pickles, let heat through well, over slow fire. Bottle while hot, lay pieces of the horseradish and some of the mustard seeds on top of each bottle. Cover and seal at once.

Tomata Catsup
From William Kitchiner, *Apicius Redivivus; Or, the Cook's Oracle*
(London, 1817)

Gather a gallon of fine, red, and full ripe tomatas; mash them with one pound of salt; let them rest for three days, press off the juice, and to each quart add a quarter of a pound of anchovies, two ounces of shallots, and an ounce of ground black pepper; boil up together for half an hour, strain through a sieve, and put to it the following spices; a quarter of an ounce of mace, the same of allspice and ginger, half an ounce of nutmeg, a drachm of coriander seed, and half a drachm of cochineal; pound all together; let them simmer gently for twenty minutes, and strain through a bag: when cold, bottle it, adding to each bottle a wineglass of brandy. It will keep for seven years.

Modern Recipes

Pickled Octopus

Contributed by Kostas Lampropoulos, Vegera Restaurant,
Mykonos, Greece

Beat the octopus on the rocks and rub it on a rough surface for about fifteen minutes, rinsing often in salt water, until it becomes soapy and foamy.

Hang the octopus in the sun and wind for three days, then grill over a low fire for ten minutes, basting with a mixture of lemon juice and olive oil. Alternatively, grill the fresh octopus over a low fire for forty minutes, turning it frequently.

Allow the grilled octopus to cool naturally – this makes it soft; then cut it into small pieces. Place the octopus in a marinade of 70 per cent red wine vinegar to 30 per cent virgin olive oil, flavoured with a small amount of dried oregano. Leave for two days before serving. To serve, dress with more virgin olive oil.

Pickled octopus keeps for one month stored in a cool place and three months refrigerated.

Shrimp
or Octopus *Escabeche*

Contributed by Brenda Garza, specialist in
nineteenth-century Mexican food

3 tbsp vegetable oil
2 onions, sliced
2 heads of garlic, cleaned and left whole
480 ml (2 cups) white vinegar
480 ml (2 cups) water
3 tsp oregano
1 tsp thyme
chillies to taste
10 whole peppercorns
1 tbsp salt

sugar to taste
1 kg (2 lb) fresh octopus or shrimps

Sauté the onion and garlic in the oil until translucent. Take off the heat and add the vinegar, water, herbs, chillies and peppercorns. Bring to the boil and add the salt. Taste; if it is too acidic, add a little sugar. Allow to cool.

Cook your shrimps or octopus in the usual way, place them in a dish and pour over the marinade. Serve cool (not chilled) or at room temperature.

Ceviche de Casarena (Acapulco Style)
Contributed by the family of Brenda Garza, Mexico

Take 1 kg (2 lb) of dorado (gilt-head bream) or wild seabass, cut into 1–2 cm (½–¾ in.) cubes. Cover the fish with the juice of about twelve large lemons and leave to cure in the refrigerator for two to three hours. Stir occasionally so that the fish cures evenly. When the fish loses its transparency, and becomes white, drain and pat dry.

Add the following ingredients combined as a sauce: 2 very ripe chopped tomatoes; ½ chopped onion; 2 tbsp ketchup; 5 tbsp orange juice; 4 tbsp apple vinegar; 2 tbsp extra virgin olive oil; 1 tsp of oregano; 1 tsp ground pepper or to taste; 6 large plain green olives; and serrano chillies finely chopped, to taste.

Pair the ceviche with chopped mango, coconut or cucumber, and accompany with fresh oysters or clams. Spicy hot sauces, ground corn tostadas and chilled tequila complete the table.

Sill i dill (Dill Herring)

Contributed by Erik Hultgren, Sweden, who has a blog devoted to
pickled herring recipes: www.skonasillar.blogspot.co.uk

100 ml (½ cup) ättiksprit (double-strength vinegar, 12%)*
200 g (1 cup) sugar
300 ml (1½ cups) water
1 can (420 g/15 oz) of herring fillets for pickling
1 bunch of dill
10 allspice berries

*If the vinegar is normal strength use 200 ml (1 cup) vinegar, 200 g
(1 cup) sugar and 200 ml (1 cup) water

Heat the vinegar, sugar and water in a saucepan until the sugar
dissolves. Let the marinade cool. Cut the herring into pieces, cut the
dill with scissors and grind the allspice coarsely. Layer the herring,
dill and allspice in a jar. Pour over the marinade to cover and put
on the lid. Allow to marinate for at least one day.

Fresh Fish Pickle from Kerala

Contributed by chef Yusuf, Ury Restaurant,
Newcastle-upon-Tyne, UK

2 kingfish steaks
1 tbsp ground turmeric
1 tbsp ground chilli powder
½ tbsp salt
½ tsp mustard seeds
2½ dry chillies
handful curry leaves
small piece fresh root ginger, finely chopped
½ small garlic bulb, finely chopped
2 onions, finely chopped
1 tbsp oil
250 ml (1 cup) water

Chop the kingfish into small pieces and fry in a little oil. Remove from the pan and mix the cooled fish with a little more oil, the turmeric powder, chilli powder and salt. Set aside.

In a separate pan, heat the remaining oil and add the mustard seeds, dry chillies and curry leaves. Stir well, add the ginger and garlic and fry until golden. Add the onions and fry for a further ten minutes until golden brown. Stir in the fish mixture and water and cook for some time. Taste and adjust the seasoning by adding more turmeric and salt.

The pickle keeps for four days stored in the fridge.

Baechu Kimchi (Cabbage Kimchi)
Contributed by Kie-Jo Sarsfield, Korean cook, food writer and blogger: www.ksarsfield.blogspot.com

2 large Korean cabbages (*baechu*) or Chinese leaves (elongated green cabbages)
500–600 g (1 lb 2 oz–1 lb 6 oz) coarse sea salt
2 *mooli* (long white radish)
300 g (11 oz) spring onions
150 g (5 oz) *gochugaru* (Korean chilli flakes)
100 g (3½ oz) Korean salted shrimps
120 ml (½ cup) Korean anchovy sauce or
Thai fish sauce
5 tbsp crushed garlic
3 tbsp grated ginger
1 tbsp sugar

You will need an airtight glass jar large enough to take two cabbages with room to spare (see recipe).

Trim the cabbage and remove any leaves that are yellow or bruised. Cut each cabbage in half. Make a slit in the white core of each half. Dissolve 300 g (11 oz) of the salt in 2 litres (8½ cups) of water. Sprinkle the remaining salt between the leaves of the cabbage. Place the salted cabbage in the salt water. Leave for two hours, turn the cabbages and leave for a further two hours. Rinse the cabbages well and drain. Taste the cabbage, if it is too salty soak in water for a further hour.

For the kimchi paste: peel the radishes and cut into long matchsticks, about 5 cm (2 in.) long and 3 mm (1/10 in.) thick. Clean the spring onions and cut to the same size as the radish. In a large bowl, place the radish, spring onion, chilli flakes, shrimps, fish sauce, garlic, ginger and sugar, mix well by hand, leave for half an hour.

Take each cabbage half in turn and place it in the bowl with the kimchi paste, smear the kimchi sauce between every leaf, working it in well. Fold the top leaves of the cabbage down over the bottom half, smooth the outside leaves around it and put in the jar. Pour over 1 cup of water and a pinch of sea salt. Press the cabbages down into the water. The jar should not be more than 80 per cent full, as liquid will be drawn from the cabbage by the salt.

Store the jar in a cool place for one to two days and then transfer to the fridge to ferment slowly. You can eat the unfermented kimchi immediately, but it is best slightly fermented, after three to four days.

Turşu (Pickled Peppers)
Contributed by Aylin Öney Tan, editor of *A Taste of Sun and Fire: Gaziantep Cookery* (Gaziantep, 2012)

2 kg (4 lb) snake cucumbers
1 kg (2 lb) small green bell peppers
480–720 ml (2–3 cups) vinegar
2.4 l (10 cups) water
120 ml (½ cup) citric acid
100 g (1 cup) coarse pickling salt

Wash and dry the snake cucumbers and peppers. Remove the tops of the snake cucumbers and cut the long ones into two or three segments. Remove the pepper stalks and pierce the bottom of each with the tip of a sharp knife. Arrange in a 5 litre (10½ pint) pickle jar. Mix the vinegar, water, citric acid and salt and pour into the jar. Make sure that the brine covers the vegetables completely.

Cover and leave in a cool dark place for several weeks. Every day press the vegetables down into the brine with a wooden spoon.

Berenjenas de Almagro (Aubergines from Almagro)
Contributed by Paloma Lendínez, who provides cookery demonstrations, including this recipe, on her YouTube channel, 'Canal cómo se hace'

1 ½ kg (3 lb) Almagro aubergines – small, immature aubergines with the outer leaves still attached
4 garlic cloves, sliced
1 tbsp sweet *pimentón*
1 tbsp cumin seeds
125 ml (½ cup) extra virgin olive oil
1 to 2 red peppers, roasted, peeled and torn
small dried fennel sticks
1 litre (4 cups) water
750 ml (3 cups) white wine vinegar
salt to taste

Wash the aubergines, make a shallow cut across the top, and place them in a saucepan, cover with water and bring to the boil. Cook for about fifteen minutes. Drain, refresh with water and set aside.

Prepare a dressing with the garlic, *pimentón*, cumin seeds and three-quarters of the olive oil, pound and blend well. Fill each aubergine with some of the red pepper and a little of the garlic and *pimentón* dressing, securing each one with a fennel stick. Place the filled aubergines in a large bowl with the rest of the dressing. Mix the water with the vinegar and rest of the olive oil and some salt and pour over the aubergines. Cover and let the aubergines rest in the fridge for three to four days. Fill small or large glass jugs with the aubergines, cover with the pickling liquid and leave to cure for a few more days.

Umeboshi (Pickled Japanese Plums)

Contributed by Voltaire Cang, modified from a family recipe
of Y. Morikawa

Ripe *ume* – Japanese plums – appear in early June, coinciding with
the start of the rainy season. The length of the rainy season determines how long the plums are pickled, which gives rise to different
umeboshi 'vintages'.

1 kg (2 1b) of yellow *ume* (Japanese plums)
150 g (5 oz) sea salt
200 ml (1 cup) approx. *shōchū* (Japanese or other vodka with at
least 35 per cent alcohol content)

Optional (to colour the plums red):
100 g (4 oz) red *shiso*/perilla leaves (*Perilla frutescens*)
3 handfuls of salt

Take the plums and remove the calyx from each with a toothpick.
Wash the plums and place in flat baskets to dry. Douse the dry
plums in *shōchū* liquor to sterilize them, drain and dredge with
the salt.

Line the pickling container with a thick food-grade plastic bag.
Fill the bag with the salted plums and lay weights on top; close the
bag and secure tightly. Store in a cool, dark place for about three
days, until the juices of the plums – *umezu* (plum vinegar) – covers
them. Remove one of the stone weights. Retie the plastic bag and
leave for two to four weeks if you are using red perilla, or until the
end of the rainy season if you are not.

Using perilla leaves: wash the leaves and drain. Mix in one
handful of salt and squeeze the leaves to remove liquid. Repeat the
process twice more. Take some plums and their liquor and place
in a bowl. Mix in the leaves. Return the plums with the leaves to
the pickling container. Retie the bag and store until the end of the
rainy season.

When the rainy season is over (mid-/late July), take the plums
from the pickling container, leaving the *umezu* behind. Lay the

plums (picking off any perilla leaves) in a single layer in flat baskets. If you have used perilla leaves strain them from the *umezu*. Spread the perilla leaves in baskets. Transfer the *umezu* to a glass container.

Take the plums, perilla leaves and *umezu* outside and place in direct sunlight to dry/sterilize. The plums must be dried in the sun for three consecutive days and three nights. Once the plums have dried, place them in dry jars sterilized with *shōchū*. To make a slightly sweet-sour *umeboshi*, a little sugar can be sprinkled on the plums. The dried perilla leaves may be stored with the *umeboshi* or separately: they are often ground into a powder for flavouring fish and vegetables. The *umezu* is retained separately and used as vinegar. *Umeboshi* last indefinitely.

References

2 Asia: Ferment and Fire

1 Mould ferments were prepared from cakes of cooked wheat or rice left to develop a powdery covering of yellow mould, typically *Aspergillus* and *Rhizopus*.
2 14 March 1967. *Foreign Relations of the United States, 1964–1968*, vol. XXIX, Part 1, Korea, Department of State, Washington, cited in *The Rushford Report Archives*, www.rushfordreport. com, 2003/4.
3 Carl S. Pederson, *Microbiology of Food Fermentations* (Westport, CT, 1979), p. 19.
4 Mark Magnier, 'In an Age of SARS, Koreans tout Kimchi Cure', www.latimes.com, 17 June 2003.
5 Laurence Oliphant, *Narrative of the Earl of Elgin's Mission to China and Japan in the Years 1857, '58, '59* (London, 1859), vol. II, Chap. VI, pp. 131–2.
6 Takeo Koizumi, 'Traditional Japanese Foods and the Mystery of Fermentation', *Food Culture*, 1 (2000), pp. 20–23 (p. 23).

3 The Mediterranean: Ancient and Modern

1 Columella, Lucius Junius Moderatus, *De re rustica* (On Agriculture), trans. E. S. Forster and Edward H. Heffer, Loeb Classical Library (Cambridge, MA, and London, 1965), vol. III, Book X, 120, www.loebclassics.com.

2 Pliny the Elder, *Naturalis historia* (Natural History), 2nd edn, trans. and ed. by H. Rackham, Loeb Classical Library (Cambridge, MA, 1968), Book XIX, 43, www.loebclassics.com.

3 Martial, *Epigrams*, ed. and trans. by D. R. Shackleton Bailey, Loeb Classical Library (Cambridge, MA, 1993), Book XIII, 83, www.loebclassics.com.

4 'The Description of Familiar Foods', trans. and introduction by Charles Perry, in *Medieval Arab Cookery*, ed. R. Maxime, A. J. Arberry and Charles Perry (Totnes, 2001), pp. 274–410 (p. 406).

4 From the Middle East to Latin America: Arabs and Conquistadores

1 Extract from Nawal Nasrallah, *Annals of the Caliphs' Kitchens: Ibn Sayyār al-Warrāq's Tenth Century Baghdadi Cookbook* (Leiden, 2010), p. 206.

2 Ibid., p. 208.

3 Extract from Charles Perry, trans., *A Baghdad Cookery Book* (Totnes, 2005), pp. 86–7.

4 Alan Davidson, ed., *The Oxford Companion to Food* (Oxford, 1999), p. 432.

5 From the Baltic to America: Sustenance and Savour

1 Cited in Renée Valeri, 'A Preserve Gone Bad or Just Another Beloved Delicacy? *Surströmming* and *Gravlax*', in *Cured, Fermented and Smoked Foods, Proceedings of the Oxford Symposium on Food and Cookery*, ed. Helen Saberi (Totnes, 2010), pp. 343–52 (p. 351).

2 John Evelyn, *Acetaria: A Discourse of Sallets* (London, 1699), p. 23.

3 Cited in Bertram Gordon, 'Fascism, the Neo-right and Gastronomy', in *Taste: Proceedings of the Oxford Symposium*

on Food and Cookery, ed. Tom Jaine (Totnes, 1987), pp. 82–97 (pp. 83–4).
4 Robert and Helen Lynd, *Middletown: A Study in American Culture* (New York, 1929), p. 156.

6 From Asia to the Atlantic: Trade and Empire

1 Jaffur Shurreef, *Qanoon-e-Islan, or the Customs of the Moosulmans of India; comprising a full and exact account of their various rites and ceremonies*. Composed under the direction of, and translated by, G. A. Herklots, 2nd edn (Madras, 1863), p. 132.
2 *Oxford English Dictionary*, from E. B., *A New Dictionary of the Terms Ancient and Modern of the Canting Crew* (London, 1690).
3 Cited in Andrew Smith, *Pure Ketchup: A History of America's National Condiment* (Columbia, SC, 1996), pp. 19 and 184.
4 TABASCO®, the Diamond and Bottle Logos, are trademarks of McIlhenny Company, registered in the U.S. and other countries.

7 Pickles Today

1 M. Battcock and S. Azam-Ali, *Fermented Fruits and Vegetables: A Global Perspective* (Rome, 1998), paras. 1.3–1.3.2, www.fao.org, accessed 29 December 2015; and Keith Steinkraus, *Handbook of Indigenous Fermented Foods* (New York, 1983).
2 D Rybaczyk-Pathak, 'Joint Association of High Cabbage/ Sauerkraut Intake at 12–13 Years of Age and Adulthood with Reduced Breast Cancer Risk in Polish Migrant Women: Results from the U.S. Component of the Polish Women's Health Study', *American Association Cancer Research: 4th Annual Frontiers Cancer Prevention Res.* (Baltimore, MD, 2005).
3 Y. H. Hui et al., eds, *Handbook of Vegetable Preservation and Processing* (Boca Raton, FL, 2003), pp. 249–55; David Chazan,

'Korean Dish May Cure Bird Flu', www.news.bbc.co.uk, 14 March 2005; Mark Magnier, 'In An Age of SARS, Koreans Tout Kimchi Cure', www.latimes.com, 17 June 2003.

4 Sook Kwin Yong et al., 'Associations of Lifestyle and Diet with the Risk of Nasopharyngeal Carcinoma in Singapore: A Case–control Study', *Chinese Journal of Cancer*, XXXVI/3 (January 2017).

5 Kevin Miller, 'Reflex Inhibition of Electrically Induced Muscle Cramps in Hypohydrated Humans', *Medicine and Science in Sports and Exercise*, XLII/5 (May 2010), pp. 953–61.

6 Carol S. Johnston and Christy L. Appel, 'Frozen Pickle Juice Reduces Mealtime Glycemia in Healthy Adults', www.fasebj.org, April 2009.

Select Bibliography

Achaya, K. T., *A Historical Dictionary of Indian Food* (Delhi, 1998)
—, *Indian Food: A Historical Companion* (Delhi, 1994)
Anon., *Manufacture of Indian Pickles, Chutneys and Morabbas* (Calcutta, 1927)
Apicius, *The Roman Cookery Book*, trans. Barbara Flower and Elisabeth Rosenbaum (London, 1958)
Battcock, M., and S. Azam-Ali, *Fermented Fruits and Vegetables: A Global Perspective*, Food and Agriculture Organization of the United Nations (Rome, 1998), www.fao.org, accessed 29 December 2015
Bilgin, Arif, and Özge Samanci, *Turkish Cuisine*, trans. *Cumhur Oranci* (Ankara, 2008)
Bottéro, Jean, *Everyday Life in Ancient Mesopotamia*, trans. Antonia Nevill (Edinburgh, 2001)
Breidt, Fred, et al., 'Fermented Vegetables', in *Food Microbiology: Fundamentals and Frontiers*, ed. M. P. Doyle and R. L. Buchanan, 4th edn (Washington, DC, 2013)
Cato, Marcus Porcius, *Liber de agricultura (On Agriculture)*, trans. W. Davis, revd H. B. Ash (London, 1954)
Chang, K. C., ed., *Food in Chinese Culture: Anthropological and Historical Perspectives* (New Haven, CT, and London, 1977)
Columella, Lucius Junius Moderatus, *De re rustica (On Agriculture)*, trans. E. S. Forster and Edward H. Heffer, vol. III, Books X–XII (Cambridge, MA, and London, 1965)
Curtis, Robert, *Ancient Food Technology* (Leiden, 2001)

Cutting, C. L., *Fish Saving: A History of Fish Processing from Ancient to Modern Times* (London, 1955)

Dalby, Andrew, *Flavours of Byzantium* (Totnes, 2003)

—, *Siren Feasts: A History of Food and Gastronomy in Greece* (London and New York, 1996)

Darby, W. J., P. Ghalioungui and L. Grivetti, *Food: Gift of Osiris*, vols I and II (London, 1977)

di Schino, June, '*Kimchi*: Ferment at the Heart of Korean Cuisine, from Local Identity to Global Consumption', in *Cured, Fermented and Smoked Food, Proceedings of the Oxford Symposium of Food and Cookery 2010*, ed. Helen Saberi (Totnes, 2011)

Dunlop, Fuchsia, *Revolutionary Chinese Cookbook: Recipes from Hunan Province* (London, 2006)

Eden, Trudy, *Cooking in America, 1590–1840* (Westport, CT, 2006)

Efendi, Turabi, *A Turkish Cookery Book: A Collection of Receipts* (London, 1865)

Hepinstall, Hi Soo Shin, *Growing Up in a Korean Kitchen* (Berkeley, CA, 2001)

Hess, Karen, transcr., *Martha Washington's Booke of Cookery* (New York, 1995)

Hosking, Richard, *A Dictionary of Japanese Food: Ingredients and Culture* (Tokyo and Rutland, VT, 1996)

Huang, H. T., *Science and Civilization in China*, vol. VI: *Biology and Biological Technology*, Part V, 'Fermentations and Food Science', part of *Science and Civilization in China*, ed. Joseph Needham (Cambridge, 2001)

Hui, Y. H., et al., eds, *Handbook of Vegetable Preservation and Processing* (Boca Raton, FL, 2003)

Ishige, Naomichi, *The History and Culture of Japanese Food* (London, 2000)

Katz, Sandor Ellix, *The Art of Fermentation: An In-depth Exploration of Essential Concepts and Processes from Around the World* (White River Junction, VT, 2012)

Leslie, (Miss), *Directions for Cookery, In Its Various Branches* (Philadelphia, PA, 1840)

Nassrallah, Nawal, *Annals of the Caliphs' Kitchens: Ibn Sayyār al-Warrāq's Tenth Century Baghdadi Cookbook* (Leiden, 2010)

Nicholson, P. T., and I. Shaw, eds, *Ancient Egyptian Materials and Technologies* (Cambridge, 2000)

Pederson, Carl, S., *Microbiology of Food Fermentations*, 2nd edn (Westport, CT, 1979)

Perry, Charles, trans., *A Baghdad Cookery Book* (Totnes, 2005)

—, trans., 'The Description of Familiar Foods: Kitāb Waṣf al-Aṭ'ima al-Mu'tāda', in R. Maxime, A. J. Arberry and Charles Perry, *Medieval Arab Cookery* (Totnes, 2001), pp. 274–410

Pettid, Michael, *Korean Cuisine* (London, 2008)

Pliny the Elder, *Naturalis historia*, trans. and ed. H. Rackham, Loeb Classical Library, 2nd edn (Cambridge, MA, 1968)

Reejhsinghani, Aroona, *Indian Pickles and Chutneys* (New Delhi, 1977)

Reynolds, Frances, 'Food and Drink in Babylonia', in *The Babylonian World*, ed. Gwendolyn Leick (London and New York, 2007), pp. 171–84

Riddervold, Astri, and Andreas Ropeid, eds, *Food Conservation* (London, 1988)

Smith, Andrew, *Pure Ketchup: A History of America's National Condiment* (Columbia, SC, 1996)

Steinkraus, Keith, *Handbook of Indigenous Fermented Foods* (New York, 1983)

Tyree, Marion Cabell, *Housekeeping in Old Virginia* (Louisville, KY, 1878)

Yerasimos, Marianna, *500 Years of Ottoman Cuisine*, trans. Sally Bradbrook (Istanbul, 2015)

Waines, David, *In a Caliph's Kitchen* (London, 1989)

Williams, Susan, *Food in the United States, 1820s–1890* (Westport, CT, and London, 2006)

Wilson, Anne, *Food and Drink in Britain* (London, 1973)

—, ed., *Waste Not, Want Not: Food Preservation in Britain from Early Times to the Present Day* (Edinburgh, 1991)

Wilson, Hilary, *Egyptian Food and Drink* (Princes Risborough, 2001)

Websites and Associations

Making Pickles

Chow Chow Pickle
www.midatlanticcooking.wordpress.com/2012/08/16/
chow-chow-pickle

Fermented Pickles
www.wildfermentation.com

'How to Make a Pickleback Cocktail', Tom Adams
www.theguardian.com

Pickles
www.sarsons.co.uk/pickling
www.bonappetit.com/test-kitchen/how-to/article/
how-to-pickle

Pickles and Chutneys
www.bbcgoodfood.com

Pickled Herrings
www.skonasillar.blogspot.co.uk

Manufacturers

Bob's Pickle Pops
www.bobspicklepops.com

Branston Pickle
www.bringoutthebranston.co.uk

Heinz
www.heinz.co.uk

Jeff's Naturals
www.jeffsnaturals.com

Lea & Perrins
www.leaandperrins.co.uk

Mt. Olive
www.mtolivepickles.com

Olive My Pickle
www.olivemypickle.com

Pickle Guys
www.pickleguys.com

The Pickle Juice Company
www.picklepower.com

Pickle Packers International
www.ilovepickles.org

Real Pickles
www.realpickles.com

Tabasco
www.tabasco.com

Museums

Heinz Exhibition, U.S.
www.heinzhistorycenter.org/exhibits/heinz

Museum Kimchikan, South Korea
www.kimchikan.com

Acknowledgements

Many people have helped me navigate the vast and complex world of pickles. I am indebted to Voltaire Cang of the RINRI Institute, Japan, Brenda Garza, specialist in nineteenth-century Mexican food, classics scholar Dr Alexandra (Sasha) Grigorieva, University of Helsinki, and Aylin Öney Tan, food writer and specialist in Anatolian food history and regional cuisines, for the time and enthusiasm they have given to this project. They have sourced material, translated recipes, offered ideas and encouragement, checked facts and more. The sections on Japan, Latin America, the Graeco-Roman period, Russia and Turkey have been greatly enriched by their knowledge. I am grateful to Naomi Tadmor for her advice on schmaltz herring, and to Vicky Hayward, journalist and author, for pointing me in the direction of Spain's unique pickled aubergine, *berenjenas de Almagro*, to María José Sevilla from Foods and Wines from Spain for finding an authentic recipe and to my colleague Alex Horsburgh who assisted with its translation. Others have read the manuscript with a critical eye and my thanks go to Professor David Feldman, Birkbeck, University of London, my partner Steven Ramm, Professor Ozge Samanci, Ottoman culinary historian at Yeditepe University, Istanbul, Professor Sami Zubaida, Birkbeck, University of London, and to Amy Salter, copy-editor at Reaktion Books. The illustrations have been sourced far and wide and credits are provided separately, but I would especially like to thank Harry Gilonis, Reaktion Books, Addie Rose Holland from Real Pickles, and Erik Hultgren, Kian Lam Kho and Jemma Watts who gave permission to use their photographs. I owe a special thank you to Michael Leaman, publisher of Reaktion Books, and Andrew F. Smith, series editor, for giving me the opportunity to tackle *Pickles* and for their guidance and patience in seeing it to fruition. Finally, I'd like to thank the cooks, chefs and families who have generously provided recipes for inclusion in this book; each has a special mention at the head of their recipe.

Photo Acknowledgements

The author and publishers wish to express their thanks to the below sources of illustrative material and/or permission to reproduce it. Some locations are also given in the captions for the sake of brevity.

Photos the author: pp. 42, 43, 48, 51, 60, 63, 66, 67, 81, 114; courtesy Bob's Pickle Pops (artist: Victor Guiza): p. 129; photo © ByeBye-Tokyo/iStock International: p. 6; from John Lewis Childs, *Childs' Rare Flowers, Vegetables and Fruits* (New York, 1903): p. 111 (photo U.S. Department of Agriculture, National Agricultural Library); photos © Cultural Heritage Administration, Republic of Korea, 2013, with the permission of UNESCO: pp. 25, 29; from William Curtis, *The Botanical Magazine, or, Flower-garden Displayed . . .*, vol. IX (London, 1795), reproduced courtesy of Biodiversity Heritage Library (www.biodiversitylibrary.org): p. 52; photo Herbert E. French/Library of Congress, Washington, DC (Prints and Photographs Division – National Photo Company Collection): p. 100; photo Brenda Garzia, reproduced by kind permission: p. 72; Gemäldegalerie Alte Meister, Dresden (photo ART Collection/Alamy Stock Photo): p. 77; photo © gontabunta/iStock International: p. 36; HJ Heinz Company Photographs, Senator John Heinz History Center: p. 123; image courtesy of HJ Heinz Foods UK Limited: p. 118; photo Heritage Image Partnership Ltd/Alamy Stock Photo: p. 41; photo Keith Homan/BigstockPhoto: p. 117 (reproduced by kind permission of Crosse & Blackwell:); photograph by Erik Hultgren (skonasillar.blogspot.com): p. 79; photo © Ishikawa Prefecture Tourism League: p. 38; Jemma Watts Photography, reproduced courtesy of Aspall:

Index

italic numbers refer to illustrations; **bold** to recipes